Festpredigten

Festpredigten

Twenty Festival Sermons
(1897–1902)

ISAAC ROSENBERG

Translated from the German by Fred Gottlieb

Copyright © Fred Gottlieb
Jerusalem 2012/5772

All rights reserved. No part of this publication may be translated, reproduced, stored in a retrieval system or transmitted, in any form or by any means, electronic, mechanical, photocopying, recording or otherwise, without express written permission from the publishers.

Cover Design Concept: Fred Gottlieb
Graphic Artist: S. Kim Glassman
Typesetting: Stephanie & Ruti Design

ISBN: 978-965-229-538-5

1 3 5 7 9 8 6 4 2

Gefen Publishing House Ltd.	Gefen Books
6 Hatzvi Street	11 Edison Place
Jerusalem 94386, Israel	Springfield, NJ 07081 USA
972-2-538-0247	1-800-477-5257
orders@gefenpublishing.com	orders@gefenpublishing.com

www.gefenpublishing.com

Printed in Israel   *Send for our free catalogue*

Library of Congress Cataloging-in-Publication Data

Rosenberg, Isaac, 1860–1940.
 [Festpredigten. English]
 Festpredigten : twenty festival sermons : 1897–1902 / by Isaac Rosenberg ; translated by Fred Gottlieb.
   p. cm.
 The sermons published in this volume were composed and delivered between the years 1897 and 1903, in Thorn, Germany, by the leader of that Jewish community, Rabbi Dr. Isaac Rosenberg. The collection was originally published in Frankfurt am Main in 1903 with the title Festpredigten, meaning "Festival Sermons" — ECIP text.
 ISBN 978-965-229-538-5 (alk. paper)
 1. Jewish festival-day sermons. I. Gottlieb, Fred. II. Title.
 BM745.R6613 2011
 296.4'53—dc23
                          2011031769

CRITICAL REVIEWS OF THE ORIGINAL PUBLICATION OF *FESTPREDIGTEN*

The following are excerpts of reviews of the original volume of sermons, written in German, from the publications *Israelitisches Familienblatt*, *Jüdische Presse*, *Der Israelit* (Nov. 15, 1903), *Jüdisches Literaturblatt*, and *Algemeine Zeitung des Judenthums*.

[There are] special demands that current times have made on the preacher because of the reduced synagogue attendance and the marked reduction in Jewish knowledge among most of his congregants. The sermon must strike a sympathetic chord that will resound among his listeners. In this, Dr. Rosenberg has succeeded admirably. He understands our times, and the threats posed to our religion.

These twenty sermons reveal a faithful shepherd transmitting to his flock admonitions and teachings drawn from the living well of life. He is aware of the needs, wishes, troubles, and delights of his people.

The author knows how to weave in an appropriate Midrashic word, a Talmudic parable, or an illuminating biblical verse in just the right place.

The language is simple, rich in poetry, without affectation. Nobility of speech, clarity, and order of construction – all of these assure these sermons a place in homiletic literature.

One would wish that this collection of sermons would find its way into every Jewish home.

Contents

Translator's Introduction ix
Author's Introduction xix

1. The Festival Angel: Rosh Hashanah Eve 5662 [1901] 1
2. Prayer: First Day Rosh Hashanah 5661 [1900] 4
3. Examining Our Wishes: First Day Rosh Hashanah 5663 [1902] 8
4. Sacrifices: Second Day Rosh Hashanah 5659 [1898] 13
5. The Ways of God: Kol Nidrei 5658 [1897] 17
6. Our Collective Responsibility: Kol Nidrei 5660 [1899] 22
7. Seeking God: Mussaf Yom Kippur 5661 [1900] 27
8. The Effect of Our Celebration: Ne'ilah 5661 [1900] 32
9. The Farewell: Ne'ilah 5662 [1901] 36
10. The Sukkah: A Representation of Life: Sukkot 5663 [1902] 39
11. Bidding the Festivals Farewell: Shemini Atzeret 5663 [1902] 43
12. Youth and Old Age: First Day Pesach 5659 [1899] 47
13. The Family Celebration: First Day Pesach 5662 [1902] 53
14. The Merit of the Pious Women: Second Day Pesach 5659 [1899] 58
15. The Jewish Heart: Seventh Day Pesach 5662 [1902] 62
16. Israel's Victory and Song: Eighth Day Pesach 5659 [1899] 66
17. The God of the Fathers: Eighth Day Pesach 5663 [1903] 71

18. The Significance of the Revelation: First Day Shavuot 5661 [1901] 75

19. Honor Your Father and Mother: Second Day Shavuot 5660 [1900] 80

20. I, the Lord, Am Your God: First Day Shavuot and Confirmation 5663 [1903] 85

Translator's Introduction

The sermons published in this volume were composed and delivered between the years 1897 and 1903, in Thorn, Germany, by the leader of that Jewish community, Rabbi Dr. Isaac Rosenberg. The collection was originally published in Frankfurt am Main in 1903 with the title *Festpredigten*, meaning "Festival Sermons." Many German rabbis at that time published their sermons, but there are very few that have been translated into English. I chose to translate the book because I believe the sermons contain messages that are relevant for us today – messages that the English reader can enjoy on a Sabbath afternoon and take to heart. The sermons will be of interest to students of homiletics and its history, and they say much about the religious observance and knowledge among contemporary German Jewry. Last but not least, I have a personal interest in the work, in that the author was my grandfather. I am happy and proud to make his name better known.

Rabbi Dr. Isaac Rosenberg, 1860–1940

Isaac Rosenberg was born on October 5, 1860, the youngest of six children, in the West German town of Rosenthal in Hessen, near the city of Kassel. He attended the Jewish Teachers' Seminary in Kassel during the years 1876 to 1879. Following two years in various teaching positions, he enrolled in the University of Marburg, where he studied Oriental philology, philosophy, and literature. His doctoral thesis, "The Aramaic Verb in the Babylonian Talmud," was published in 1887 under the auspices of the University of Leipzig.

In 1884 Isaac Rosenberg entered the University of Berlin, and at the same time enrolled at the Rabbiner-Seminar in Berlin (Hildesheimer Seminary). He was ordained as a rabbi in 1888. All graduates of the Rabbiner-Seminar had academic degrees of Ph.D. or were Ph.D. candidates. They constituted a new class of rabbis known as "Rabbiner Doktor," and their training at the seminary was particularly aimed at enabling them to go out into the nonreligious communities and speak to their flock in the modern German idiom.[1]

Rosenberg's first pulpit was in the Berlin suburb of Brandenburg, where he officiated between 1888 and 1892. During the next twenty-five years he was district rabbi in the eastern German city of Thorn, serving also the surrounding Jewish communities. When Thorn was annexed to Poland following World War I, Rosenberg moved with his family to Berlin, where he served both as teacher and as inspector of Hebrew schools for another eighteen years. Shortly after Kristallnacht he fled to England, where he died on February 2, 1940. He is buried just outside of London.

The years of the turn of the twentieth century, during which the sermons in this volume were composed, would seem to have been happy ones. The Jewish population of Thorn was at its peak, and Isaac Rosenberg was well ensconced as a leader in his community. He was blessed with three sons and a daughter. The later years were not so kind to him. The number of Jews in Thorn began to dwindle, as did their religious observance. Rosenberg yearned for the richer cultural life in Berlin. By the time he was able to obtain a position in Berlin, his second oldest son had succumbed to tuberculosis. Another son died of leukemia a decade later, shortly after settling in Palestine. It was his oldest son and his youngest child, a daughter, who together presented him with five grandchildren. At the time of this writing, his progeny extends into the fifth generation and, together with their spouses, exceeds well over one hundred souls, all Jewish, all Torah-true.[2]

---

1 *Encyclopedia Judaica*, 13:1459 (Jerusalem: Macmillan, 1971).
2 Fred Gottlieb, *My Opa: The Diary of a German Rabbi* (Jerusalem: Mazo Publishers, 2005).

Thorn

The city of Thorn (it became Toruń after it was annexed by Poland following World War I) was located at the German-Polish border. Jews first settled there in 1793, but they were limited to only certain areas, and their subsistence was very meager. It was only in the second part of the nineteenth century that Jews received official permission to settle in Thorn, and the number of businessmen, lawyers, and physicians increased. The synagogue was erected in 1847, which was also the year in which the local Jews were emancipated and granted full citizenship.

For a period of fifty years, the towering figure in Thorn was Zevi Hirsch Kalischer, author of *Derishat Ziyyon*. Kalischer died in 1874, eighteen years before Rosenberg assumed the pulpit there. The end of the nineteenth century saw the Jewish population of Thorn reach its height, at 1,371 people, or about 5 percent of the population. The community decreased in size dramatically after World War I and disappeared entirely after 1939.[3]

Isaac Rosenberg's Sermons

In the course of his rabbinic career, Isaac Rosenberg composed thousands of sermons – sermons for the synagogue on Sabbaths and festivals, as well as for weddings, circumcisions, bar mitzvahs, and funerals – in Thorn as well as in the surrounding Jewish communities. Their composition and delivery became a special passion of his, and he recorded in his diary the specific biblical text upon which each week's sermon was based. He firmly believed that sermons must be memorized and delivered without notes as a way of conveying the preacher's sincerity. With unintended humor, he subjected each sermon to critical evaluation, each sermon called "superb" or "very well received."[4] In fact, reviews of this volume in Jewish newspapers at the time of publication were uniformly favorable in their praise for the clarity, style, elegance, and content of the sermons.[5]

---

3   *Pinkas Hakehillot Polin* (Jerusalem: Yad Vashem, 5759/1999).
4   Gottlieb, *My Opa*.
5   *Der Israelit, Central Organ für das orthodoxe Judenthum*, November 16, 1903.

Among the early influences on Rosenberg's style of preaching was Azriel Hildesheimer, founder and head of the Rabbiner-Seminar, who, among others, delivered lectures on homiletics.[6] A rich source of homiletics was the extensive 1890 manual by Sigmund Maybaum,[7] a docent at the Lehranstalt für die Wissenschaft des Judenthums in Berlin (Reform). A perusal of Rosenberg's *Festival Sermons* suggests that he was familiar with this work. An equally extensive treatise on homiletics by Joseph Wohlgemuth (Orthodox) was published at the time that the sermons in this volume were delivered.[8] Since this was a supplement to a yearbook from the Rabbiner-Seminar, Rosenberg must have been well acquainted with this publication as well as its author.

Religious Observance in Germany in the Nineteenth Century

Normative Judaism was once defined by adherence to halachah, and autonomous Jewish communities had the power to excommunicate deviants. By the early decades of the nineteenth century, enforcing religious observance on individuals was no longer possible because of the great number of Jews who, for economic or political reasons, chose not to observe such basic Jewish laws as the Sabbath or kashrut. In parallel, German states had begun to suspend Jewish communal authority regarding the religious behavior of its members. By the mid-nineteenth century, non-observant Jews were in the majority, and by the end of World War I, only 20 percent of the German Jewish population was Orthodox.[9] Nevertheless, nonobservant Jews were accepted and counted as part and parcel of Jewish society on the basis of the principle that "An Israelite, even if he has sinned, remains an Israelite."[10] A perusal of the twenty sermons included in this book makes it clear that in virtually all of them, Rosenberg

---

6 Annual Report of the Rabbiner-Seminar, 1884.

7 Sigmund Maybaum, *Jüdische Homiletik* (Berlin: Ferd. Dümmlers Verlagsbuchhandlung, 1890).

8 Joseph Wohlgemuth, *Beiträge zu einer jüdischen Homiletik*, Annual Report of the Rabbiner-Seminar 1903–1904.

9 Adam S. Ferziger, *Exclusion and Hierarchy* (Philadelphia: University of Pennsylvania Press, 2005).

10 Talmud Bavli, *Sanhedrin* 44a.

was addressing Jews whose attachment to religious observance had become very tenuous, but from his perspective they all remained Jews in the eyes of God.

Realizing that compliance with rabbinic decisions could no longer be coerced, Orthodox rabbis had to take a more lenient approach in enforcing many halachic matters, lest they turn individuals still further away from Judaism. They were most reluctant to compromise regarding Sabbath observance, dietary laws, and family purity, but even with Sabbath observance, some authorities felt that enforcing strictures might cause yet further estrangement.[11] Rosenberg's Second Day Pesach 5659 sermon suggests such leniency for the breadwinner, in his struggle for existence, who violates the Sabbath but finds warmth and comfort upon his return to his Jewish home.

The *Predigt*

Until the early nineteenth century, the traditional form of sermon was called the "*drashah*." It was delivered in Hebrew or Yiddish and directed to an audience that was knowledgeable in Bible and Talmud. The preachers were not necessarily the community rabbis, nor were the sermons always a part of the synagogue service. Only three times yearly did community rabbis regularly preach: on the Sabbath before Pesach (Shabbat Hagadol), the Sabbath between Rosh Hashanah and Yom Kippur (Shabbat Shuvah), and on Yom Kippur.

Changing factors, including the Emancipation, the decline of both Jewish knowledge and religiosity in the nineteenth century, and the Reform movement, brought about a new type of sermon in Germany, the Predigt. Unlike the drashah, the Predigt was delivered in the German vernacular, expressing values in a contemporary idiom, and it became a regular part of the synagogue service. (It was Reform Judaism, not Orthodox, that considered the sermon to be an integral part of the service.) A biblical text was developed into a central theme, which emphasized edification of the listener rather than instruction and admonition. In this vein, it was directed more toward the emotion than the intellect, and preachers saw it as a means of strengthening the waning

---

11 Ferziger, *Exclusion and Hierarchy*.

religious spirit of its listeners. "Religion" rather than religious observance was emphasized, and this indeed characterizes most of Isaac Rosenberg's sermons.

The Predigt clearly found its Jewish roots in the preaching of the Reform, who consciously modeled their sermons on the pattern of Christian homiletics.[12] In some communities, the use of the vernacular (High German) was a particular point of objection, especially where the older type of rabbi-preacher was unfamiliar with the modern idiom. However, it was realized that addressing the people in the language they commonly used offered the best potential for reaching the more estranged Jews, and could serve as an effective way to stem the tide toward Reform and conversion to Christianity. In addition, during the French occupation of parts of Germany (1807–1813), the Napoleonic Consistory made the use of the vernacular mandatory. Such Orthodox luminaries as Jacob Ettlinger and Samson Raphael Hirsch preached effectively in German, which may also have increased synagogue attendance by women and led to their more active involvement in communal affairs.[13] To the objection that the Predigt was a non-Jewish institution, Leopold Zunz countered, in his book *Gottesdienstlische Vorträge*,[14] that the sermon is deeply rooted in ancient Jewish tradition and antedated Christianity.

With the founding of the Rabbiner-Seminar in Berlin, homiletics became a systemized discipline and a standard course in modern rabbinical schools.[15]

Homiletic Literature

Like many of his German colleagues, Isaac Rosenberg published not only this collection of sermons as well as individual sermons for festivals (called "*statutarisch*"), but also sermons for other occasions (called "*casual*"), such as dedications, ceremonies for the swearing-in of soldiers prior to their induction

---

12 Maybaum, *Jüdische Homiletik Ferd. Dümmlers Verlagsbuchhandlung.*

13 Mordechai Breuer, *Modernity within Tradition* (New York: Columbia University Press, 1992).

14 Leopold Zunz, *Die gottesdienstlischen Vorträge der Juden historisch entwickelt* (Berlin: A. Asher, 1832).

15 Breuer, *Modernity within Tradition.*

into the military, or the celebration of the Kaiser's birthday.[16] With the exception of halachic writings, traditional homiletics had already become the most significant branch of Jewish literature in the seventeenth and eighteenth centuries, a repository of Jewish ideas, theology, and philosophy. There was hardly a Jewish community in Eastern Europe that did not produce preachers whose sermons were printed.

Style and Content of These Twenty Festival Sermons

The twenty sermons in this volume were first published in Frankfurt am Main in 1903, and they share certain basic characteristics. Each is introduced by a biblical text or by a description of the festival being celebrated. Once this has been elaborated, the listener is asked to focus on one particular aspect, which then becomes the main theme of the sermon. An attempt is made to show its relation to contemporary times and especially to contrast the actions of the biblical personalities with the audience that is being addressed. Such comparisons are not always favorable. For example, after hearing an extensive discussion on how the righteousness of the Jewish women in Egypt helped bring about the final redemption, the women in the audience are pointedly asked whether they can feel themselves fitting into the mold of these Jewish women. The reader is constantly aware of the weakness of religious commitment of the audience that is being addressed, and of the contrast between the sanctity of the time and place of the sermon versus the secular nature of the outside world. The preacher tries valiantly to have his people carry some of this holiness with them into their everyday lives. These sermons reveal the intense love of the preacher for his flock, as he makes it clear that even those attending synagogue once a year on Yom Kippur are part and parcel of the Jewish people.

One of the basic aims of the standard Predigt was spiritual elevation of the audience rather than admonition. Not so these sermons, most of which contain direct or indirect admonition. But the reproof administered is always gentle and loving, with no trace of anger, and is often accompanied by a plea to return to religion. "Religion" is indeed a term that is frequently used and is quite

---

16 Gottlieb, *My Opa*.

obviously ambiguous. The impression is that concrete mitzvot (commandments) cannot be imposed on this audience. Even the call for increased prayer is couched in vague, abstract terms. Only rarely does Rosenberg specify such active deeds as attendance in the synagogue or observing the Sabbath.

Rosenberg is a staunch defender of Orthodox Judaism, and he speaks out boldly against Reform. In his sermon showing the beautiful harmony between the young and the old, he decries apostasy for the sake of improving one's position, since it severs the intergenerational relationship. He criticizes those who disparage our religion and who question the unity of God. He reminds those who claim that morality and ethics are Christian teachings that it is Judaism that first transmitted these values to all religions, including, as Rosenberg calls it, the "daughter religion."

The language of these sermons is beautiful throughout, and often waxes poetic. An example is the sermon of the first day of Pesach 5662, which pairs the physical awakening of nature at springtime, as depicted in Song of Songs, with the stirring of the Jewish spirit at the time of the redemption from Egypt. Ample use is made of synonymous phrases to bring out certain points, although the English language does not always lend itself to translating such similar, consecutive phrases.

Several of these sermons lead into the Yizkor (Memorial) service. They serve to ask the listeners to emulate their beloved departed, and perhaps to hold on to the little religiosity that is left. There is also a frequent refrain that the Yizkor service is the constant bond, extending beyond the grave, that binds the living to the dead even years after the separation.

Confirmation

The sermon on Shavuot 5663 needs special consideration because it includes the controversial confirmation ceremony. Confirmation originated with the Reform in the early nineteenth century. It bore the characteristics of the Protestant confirmation, including the confirmand's profession of faith, as well as material concerning the principles of Reform Judaism. This was based on the model of Christian catechism. In one particular Reform ceremony, the recital of the Thirteen Articles of Faith of Maimonides constituted the profession of faith. The poem "*Yigdal*" (a poetic rendition of Maimonides' creed) was chosen as the appropriate text but, in the spirit of Protestant tradition, was sung to the melody of a popular Christmas carol!

Confirmation was intended as a personal assumption of religious duty to which the child had already been bound at birth. It was considered by the Reform as a suitable substitute for the somewhat discredited bar mitzvah, in which a boy read from the Torah in a language he did not understand and which lacked relevance to his present or future life. At the same time confirmation was suited for girls as well.

The ceremony was attacked by the Orthodox not only because of its Reform origins, but because it has no roots in Jewish tradition, and because it is the obligation of keeping Torah precepts rather than a profession of faith that constitutes the induction of a child as a full member of the community. Nevertheless it was adopted by some Orthodox congregations.[17] In addition, Jewish communities were forced by governments of the Protestant German states to introduce confirmation even against their will. Such a decree was enacted by the Westphalian Consistory in 1821.[18]

Rosenberg's confirmation ceremony was for girls only, and was performed, as was customary, on the festival of Shavuot. His diary indicates that the confirmation followed many weeks of preparation on the part of the girls. The lax state of religious observance in his community may have been a factor in choosing to maintain this custom. Rosenberg had indeed become very disappointed with the bar-mitzvah ceremony as practiced then, complaining in one of his sermons that it is more often the end rather than the beginning of a life of religious observance.

The format of Rosenberg's confirmation ceremony appears to be taken out of Maybaum's manual, and includes *Wahlsprüche*, or mottos pronounced individually by each confirmand. These were not intended to be utterances

---

17 Breuer, *Modernity within Tradition*.
18 Klaus Herrmann, "Jewish Confirmation Sermons in 19th-Century Germany," in *Preaching in Judaism and Christianity*, ed. Alexander Deeg, Walter Homolka, and Heinz-Günther Schöttler (Berlin: Walter de Gruyter, 2008), pp. 91–112.

of faith but rather expressions of ideals and ethics by which the girls were choosing to live their lives.

Rosenberg's sermon ends with the priestly blessing, which might have simply been a means of blessing – *segnen* – the youngsters. Alternatively, it might have meant "Einsegnen," meaning "consecration" or "confirmation," a part of the bar-mitzvah ceremony in Reform synagogues, whereby the rabbi would raise his hand and pronounce the priestly blessing – an innovation not practiced among the Orthodox.

Isaac Rosenberg's Publications

In addition to his homiletic writings and his doctoral thesis, Isaac Rosenberg published some of the many lectures he delivered on various occasions, two major manuals on the methodology of Jewish education,[19] and an essay comparing Goethe's Faust with Ecclesiastes. The latter was recently published in a revised English translation.[20]

Acknowledgments

In preparing this book I received invaluable assistance from Dr. David Stein, Rabbi Dr. Adam Ferziger, Professor David Halivni, Rabbi Dovid Cohen, and Dr. Daniel Gottlieb. Their contributions are gratefully acknowledged.

Fred Gottlieb, M.D.
Jerusalem 5772

---

19 J. Rosenberg, *Methodik des jüdischen Religionsunterricht* (Berlin: C. Boas Nachfolger, 1924).

20 Isaac Rosenberg, "Koheleth and Goethe's Faust," *Jewish Bible Quarterly* 37, no. 2 (April–June 2009): pp. 103–112.

Author's Introduction

The preacher can draw gratification from his work to the extent that his sermons meet a happy reception on the part of his audience. Rather than just finding approval, the preacher is concerned that his teachings make a spiritual impression that will have a lasting effect on the religious life of his audience. This can, however, be achieved only if the sermon awakens in the listener some ethical satisfaction. And yet, the spoken word tends to be forgotten, and life's demands often drive away impulses received under the influence of a sacred hour in a sacred place. I therefore wish to use the printed word to sow the seeds for renewed spiritual growth, such as the spoken sermon was able to plant into the heart. This collection of sermons should, in the first place, serve as an uplifting force in my community. And yet I do not wish to set limits to the dissemination of these sermons. I would be all the happier if they would find favor in wider circles, bringing elation and stimulation, especially if my colleagues would accept these sermons with favor.

Should my efforts meet with approval, I would consider it a stimulus to publish more of my collection of sermons, especially those preached on the Sabbath and on special occasions. In submitting these sermons for publication, it is my hope that they will find their way into people's hearts.

Thorn, August 1903
Isaak Rosenberg

The Festival Angel

Rosh Hashanah Eve 5662 [1901]

שלום עליכם מלאכי השרת מלאכי עליון.
Peace unto you, ministering angels, messengers of the Most High.
(Sabbath hymn)

With this greeting, so familiar to every religious family, let us bid welcome today not only to the holy Sabbath, but also extend our devotion to that other messenger of God now entering into our midst. Peace, in the first place, to you, the Sabbath angel, who time and again brings replenishment and tranquility into the midst of our turbulent existence and our life's struggle. And peace unto you, angel of Rosh Hashanah, as you open for us a new chapter in our lives. We greet you both, sublime messengers of God, sent by our benign Father in Heaven to uplift us spiritually and to bless us with good fortune.

More than greeting the new year, we must now also bid farewell to a trusted companion: the year that has just expired and that has accompanied us along a significant span of our lives. Our feelings mirror those of our forefather Jacob, on his way home from a strange land where he had tarried for many years. In the darkness of night, on a desolate field, a "man" wrestled with him, trying to overcome and subdue him. Only at daybreak did he desist. However, Jacob would not allow this "man" to leave, calling to him with the words לא אשלחך כי אם ברכתני, "I will not let you go until you have blessed me" (Genesis 32:27). These are our sentiments today, my listeners. We are reluctant to send forth the old year before we recall the many blessings it bestowed upon us, blessings that will continue to be a source of spiritual comfort as we enter this new phase of our lives.

O, how manifold are our hearts' sentiments tonight, as we look back at the year just gone by. For many of us, much has vanished, irrevocably lost.

Very few of us escaped unscathed in life's struggle, be it only a colleague or trusted acquaintance collapsing before our eyes, a victim of the times – no one remained completely untouched. And when we have lost some of the joy of our existence, and life becomes a vale of tears, the breast burdened with pain and bitter misfortune, we think back to last year's beginnings when we still had full possession of our loved ones. Their absence has left a void. And, alas, a survey of our own congregation evokes in us feelings of sadness: how often did hot tears, caused by bitter pain, flow down pale cheeks, as sorrow and mourning entered a previously happy home? We look around us in this house of God and we miss many a true friend and dear companion who once graced our congregation.

Nevertheless, my dear ones, היום קדוש לה׳ – "Today is holy for the Lord your God" (Nehemiah 8:9). Let us therefore not be overcome by a melancholy mood! Did we indeed see only sadness during the past year? Did not the radiance of God's sun also shine on us, allowing us to experience goodness and happiness in rich measure? All of us, even those bent with sorrow and sadness, have come to know that the Guardian of Israel neither slumbers nor sleeps, that God watches from His throne on high and protects us. As we consider all the good that God has bestowed upon us, our feelings echo those of our ancestor Jacob: קטנתי מכל החסדים ומכל האמת אשר עשית את עבדך, "I am too unworthy of all the mercies and all the truth that You have done unto Your servant" (Genesis 32:11).

Let us then not send forth the angel of the old year until he has blessed us – blessed us with the realization that in the midst of the frailty of our existence, there is a Shield and Protector on high. Let that angel not depart until he has imbued us with the unshakeable resolve to place our trust in Him Who rules over all, to cling to Him with all our heart and soul as we set out on this new year's journey. We look up to Him in trust, the all-benevolent God, Who will lead us safely along the highway of life, granting us blessing and welfare.

Imbued with these sentiments, we look to You, benevolent God on high. Gaze down with favor upon us, as we seek, in our despair, Your support. Escort and protect us as we walk along this new road of life. Do not permit us to sin or to stumble – support us by Your love. Maintain our precious family members, who constitute the joy of our lives. Guard them from illness, affliction, and worry, so that we may count them as ours for the next year, spiritually uplifted and rejoicing in the grace that You have bestowed upon us. For the parents, preserve their children, guarantors of Your grace; grant them perseverance and strength that they may learn to honor You. For the children, preserve their parents so that they might lead them to dedicate themselves to Your service and to the glorification of Your name. O, bless us all, who are assembled here; bless our families, be they near or far. Bless our entire congregation, bless our Fatherland, and bless, in Your kindness and love, all of Israel.

May these words, which I now invoke from the bottom of my heart to all assembled here, find fulfillment in their truest sense. לשנה טובה תכתבו – May this new year be a blessing for all of you. Amen.

Prayer

First Day Rosh Hashanah 5661 [1900]

ברוך א-להים אשר לא הסיר תפלתי וחסדו מאתי.
Blessed is God, Who has not withdrawn my prayer
nor His kindness from me. (Psalms 66:20)

The sentiments expressed in these words by the psalmist inspire us today, as we all, collectively, gather in the house of God on this sublime festival. We come here deeply moved as we bid farewell to the old year and embark on the extensive journey of the new year. Our hearts are troubled by an abundance of conflicting sentiments. The past has disappeared irrevocably and is no longer ours. And yet, the memory of it lives on – in what we were offered, in what we learned, the happy as well as the sad that it brought us. As we now face the future we are anxious concerning what fate life holds in store for us, and our feelings oscillate between happy expectations and uneasy despair. As we enter the holy spaces of this house of God, it is our hope that we may once regain our inner equilibrium.

We can liken ourselves to that pious woman that today's Haftarah describes so beautifully: Hannah, wife of Elkanah from the tribe of Ephraim, suffered great sorrow. Her heart was saddened because God withheld from her that ultimate joy of any wife – she had no children. Though Elkanah sought to comfort her with kind words of reassurance, Hannah did not find the peace she so very much needed. She therefore proceeded to the sanctuary and prayed to God. Her prayer was silent, but most fervent. And her prayer, though answered by the Creator only later on, had an immediate result. "Go in peace, and may the God of Israel answer your supplication," said the priest Eli, who had watched her pray and had first thought her to be intoxicated. And Hannah did go in peace because her sorrow dissipated once she had poured out her heart before God: ופניה לא היו לה עוד, "No longer was her countenance sad" (I Samuel 1:17–18).

My devout listeners: We also seek to lighten our spirits via the medium of prayer. Perhaps I speak for all of you as you cast your glance heavenward: we find an inner comfort in turning to God. Although the past evokes many sad memories, reminding us of the transient nature of our lives, and though the future is still veiled for us, our prayers allow the sunshine of God's kindness to shine through the dark clouds and into our hearts. We then sense the gratitude that the psalmist feels toward his Creator for giving him the ability to pray. Indeed, fortunate are those who maintain and cherish this ability. They do not feel forsaken, nor do they despair, knowing that a loving God watches over them, and fate no longer holds its terror.

Today, as we contemplate the blessed effect that prayer has on our spiritual well-being, let us examine the bold declaration in our Mussaf prayer: תשובה תפילה וצדקה מעבירין את רוע הגזרה, "Repentance, prayer, and charity avert the evil decree." This indicates the great importance and value of prayer in ennobling our lives and strengthening us in our struggles.

My devout listeners: a Talmudic adage (Talmud Bavli, *Yevamot* 64a) reads, קב״ה מתאוה לתפלתן של צדיקים – "God desires the prayers of the righteous, and finds pleasure therein." Indeed, there is no better indicator of our religious thinking, nor does anything bear greater testimony to our relationship to God, than our prayers to Him. Whoever recognizes God as the source of all life, aware that His love for us is that of a father for his child – he cannot but wish to draw even closer to Him, and lay out his sorrows and his joys before Him.

Thus have people prayed at all times, and we may very well assume, without the gift of prophecy, that never will humanity be without prayer. And while our concept of the Supreme Being will always be wanting, and nations will inexplicably choose gods from among the animals, prayer will always be the bearer of our innermost emotions. How was prayer first established in Israel's midst? We might say that Israel is the People of Prayer, a model for all of humanity. We taught the nations how to invest their feelings with holiness and purity. Can any human emotion of exceeding joy or abject sorrow find better expression than what is articulated in the book of Psalms? It is there that the entire spectrum of human emotion speaks to us, and every tone resonating from our heartstrings finds its meaningful echo in this book. As David and the other known and unknown psalmists prayed with great fervor, so did Israel pray since the earliest of times.

We marvel at the boldness of Abraham's intercession on behalf of the sinful inhabitants of Sodom. Alone in a solitary field in the still of the night, Jacob, while fleeing from Esau, prayed fervently that God might protect him and return him safely to his home. And that incomparable man of God – Moses! How passionately did he supplicate the Almighty, presenting his requests before God's throne, interceding for a sinful people that had made a Golden Calf, praying for his ill sister, or pleading that he be allowed to enter the Promised Land – his unshakable trust in the goodness of God is in evidence everywhere. So did Hannah pray, as our Haftarah describes; so did Solomon pray on inaugurating the Holy Temple; and thus do we also pray – when our hearts burst out in jubilation or when our souls are heavy with grief, we seek the fatherly bosom of our Creator. Though words may fail us, our hearts speak to God.

Need a mother, anxiously keeping vigil at her sick baby's crib, be taught how to pray? Will not the head of a household, consumed with worry over how to support his family by honorable means, seek God's encouragement and confidence?

That exalted prayer for help, "Do not forsake me, O God" (Psalms 38:22), is no less pleasing to God than Moses' plea for his stricken sister: א-ל נא רפא נא לה, "Please, O God, heal her" (Numbers 12:13).

Nevertheless, my devout listeners, our religion requires prayers beyond those that spring spontaneously from the depths of our hearts. Our sages have prescribed and laid out prayers that we are obligated to follow. If we scrutinize these prayers, we must come to the conclusion that they offer the most solid support for our lives.

However, the impulse to pray does not always intrude into our busy lives, concerned as we are with everyday affairs. Rarely do we lift our thoughts above the mundane to direct our glance heavenward. It is here that our religion comes to our aid. Prayer should become habitual, an ever-imperative urge, refreshing the soul just as food and drink maintain the body, and fortifying ourselves against the temptations of evil that daily seek to seduce us from the ways of virtue.

How protective and ennobling is the influence of prayer, a touchstone for the purity of our thoughts, uplifting us toward a more intimate union with the Holy One above.

Yet one more thought: our reflections here have shown us that the ability to pray is a gift from Heaven. Let us then never fail to avail ourselves of this precious gift. It is like a tender twig implanted into the soft human heart, which, without nursing, will wilt and wither. But when it is protected and cultivated, it will flourish and refresh us with its blossoms, revive us with its fruits, gathering strength and growing into a mighty tree that no wind can shake.

Only if we ourselves pray can we teach our children to pray. By accustoming them to daily prayer, we fortify them against the many temptations that life presents. And when one day they leave their parental home to face the struggles of our existence, we can feel assured about them, knowing that the scriptural passage from Isaiah 57:19 applies to them: בורא ניב שפתים שלום שלום לרחוק ולקרוב אמר ה׳ ורפאתיו, when the fruit of the lips – that is, prayer – exerts its effect, there is true peace for those who are close to us and for those who are distant. And if ever they may have been remiss before God, they will never be completely estranged, but always find their way back to Him. Amen.

Examining Our Wishes

First Day Rosh Hashanah 5663 [1902]

> והיה ביום ההוא יתקע בשופר גדול ובאו האבדים בארץ אשור והנדחים
> בארץ מצרים והשתחוו לה' בהר הקדש בירושלים.
> It shall be on that day that a great shofar shall sound and those who
> are lost in the land of Assyria and those cast away in the land of
> Egypt will come, and they will prostrate themselves to the Lord on
> the holy mountain in Jerusalem. (Isaiah 27:13)

With this unrestrained flight of fancy, in which the remotest of times assume form and reality, the prophet Isaiah envisions a sublime wonder that will come to pass. The scattered remnants of Israel, residing in the land of Assyria and tarrying in Egypt, will ascend, united as one people, to Jerusalem, there to serve God on His holy mountain.

והיה ביום ההוא, "And it shall be on that same day," says the prophet. Distant, very distant, is that time which his prophecy sees so clearly, and so is it far away for us. Millennia may yet pass before this prophetic ideal will come to fulfillment in all its brilliance, and that for which we so yearn will become reality. Nevertheless, on this our solemn festival, as the congregations of Israel assemble piously before the presence of God, we perceive a reflection of some of the splendor of this prophetic vision. On this day, as we listen to the sound of the shofar, those who have lost their way and gone astray come to prostrate themselves before the eternal God. They all find their way back who count themselves among us and in whose hearts there glows a spark of Jewish feeling.

What is it that affects us so deeply as the New Year draws nigh? What directs our gaze and our thoughts heavenward today more than at other times? Has the sun ascended the firmament today with greater brilliance, or is the earth adorned with more luscious greenery? Is there an unusual natural phenomenon that drives our innermost selves to worship the Creator? One glance outside will indicate that all is the same. No, it is we who are transformed. We feel different today as our thoughts are, instinctively, elevated to greater heights of holiness.

The past lies behind us, irrevocably vanished. The future looms before us with no guarantees, and we are made more acutely aware of the frailty of our earthly existence. Fearful of what is to come, we seek refuge in the proximity to God, Who is exalted beyond anything transitory or changing and Who will support us in our weakness. In prayer we approach God's countenance, humble in the awareness of our insignificance. Deeply moved, we present our wishes before the throne of glory. As always in life, when we are wanting in ability and in strength, we seek refuge in our wishes, be they justified or not, worthy of fulfillment or deserving of condemnation.

Especially on this day, then, it behooves us to consider carefully the consequences of our hopes and desires, since what we wish is what we strive for, and what we strive for is what shapes our existence. On this day of Rosh Hashanah, our religion bids us examine and take stock of our lives so that we may be judged worthy and pious. If we seek, on this festival, to shape for ourselves a future rich in blessing, we must think carefully about what we seek. We will then realize whether the path of our life is directed toward ennoblement and perfection, or whether we risk losing our way in life's aberrations.

Today, we will center our remarks around the verse from Scripture: משפט נבחרה לנו נדעה בינינו מה טוב, "Let us choose for ourselves what is right; let us know among ourselves what is good" (Job 34:4).

I.

רבות מחשבות בלב איש ועצת ה' היא תקום – "Many designs are in a man's heart, but only the counsel of God will prevail" (Proverbs 19:21). This is indeed our everyday experience. Plans, thoughts, and designs rage within our minds. One man's demands cost another his position; fulfillment of one man's wish takes another one's rightful place. The Midrash states, אין אדם מת וחצי תאותו בידו, "No man ever sees even half of his wishes fulfilled" (*Ecclesiastes Rabbah* 1).

And how much distress, discontent, and strife is evoked by unfulfilled desires? Yes, all the misery residing among people, all sorrow and sadness depressing the spirit – where is its origin if not in the gloom of unfulfilled wishes? The discord that disrupts families, envy causing incitement of entire social classes one against the other, and jealousy depriving other people of their happiness – from whence do they derive their destructive influence if not on the basis of untamed, unbridled, and unfulfilled wishes?

Nevertheless our ability to wish is a precious and sublime gift from God. For everything noble and beautiful, all progress and culture, all that embellishes and advances mankind – we owe to that insatiable longing for self-improvement, the constant striving to make our existence more worthy, our lives more beautiful, and our living conditions more gratifying. And when we ourselves have achieved success, esteem, honor, and recognition – what is it that allows us no repose? What lends us endurance and steels our energy, if not the urge to climb yet higher in the ranks of human society? And yet, while our wishes can leave us greatly elevated, they can also thoroughly debase us. Where then is the dividing line between one wish and another? It is so indistinct as to be barely recognizable. So easily can a wish intended for our welfare become an agony and a curse. How appropriate then is the reminder: משפט נבחרה לנו נדעה ביננו מה טוב, "Let us choose for ourselves what is right; let us know among ourselves what is good."

In the meantime we must pose the question: Do you presume to know what is really good for your welfare and worthwhile striving for? May your wishes be fulfilled! And yet, while these wishes may appear to you to be beneficial, are they truly consistent with what is good and correct? Look back at the past! Have you asked only for what your conscience deemed to be good, never yearning for what is selfish and unjustifiable in the eyes of the Almighty – or have you wished for what might bring passing joy to you but ultimate harm to others?

You might have felt aggrieved when your wishes remained unfulfilled, perhaps even complaining to God that fate has treated you unfairly. And yet even now your heart may long for what may bring you one disappointment after another, cause discord in your soul, and diminish your trust in God –

wishes that cannot and should not be fulfilled. Be advised, therefore, to evaluate your desires, and measure them by what is right and just, and beneficial for your fellow man.

The teachings of the past are well worth considering. You have attained much of what you thought to be beneficial in achieving your life's goal, while other wishes, no less urgent, have yet to be realized. But tell me honestly, has the fulfillment of your dreams really made you happier and brought you more contentment than what you had in past years? Be aware, then, that what seems beneficial at the moment may later prove not to have nearly the value that we attributed to it. Our religion teaches us that only that which is true and noble has lasting worth and merits our efforts in its pursuit. Directing our wishes in this way, we comply with the verse משפט נבחרה לנו נדעה בינינו מה טוב, "Let us choose for ourselves what is right, let us know among ourselves what is good."

II.

While our preoccupation and prayers on this festival are with the future of our own lives, our own lifestyles, and our own means of support, our religion seeks to broaden our horizons to include others in our prayers. Not that we are to suppress our natural sentiments of praying for welfare, blessing, good health, fortune, and prosperity. But we are made to realize, at the same time, that we belong not just to our family, but that we are part and parcel of the broader community, that we are a part of humanity, and that we are Jews.

Indeed the first two requests in the principal prayer of the New Year are directed toward this goal. We pray to the All-Merciful that He may instill the recognition and fear of the Lord in all His creatures, that the realm of piety and virtue be extended, that love and good will take continually deeper roots, and that all humanity join in one alliance of peace – this constitutes the first request that we direct to our Creator in the Amidah of Rosh Hashanah. Yea, may they all come, those outside who vex us by their lack of kindness, who pursue us hatefully, and who falsely accuse us of blatant selfishness – let them come and hear that Israel, on this their holiest and most solemn day, pray in the first place for the welfare, enlightenment, and ennoblement of all of humanity.

Even when our hearts are heavily burdened with worries and concerns, our faith directs us to higher aspirations, teaching us to consider others as well as ourselves.

From concern for humanity in general, we now direct our thoughts to the community of Israel: ובכן תן כבוד ה' לעמך תהלה ליראיך ותקוה טובה לדורשיך, "Give honor, O God, to Your people, esteem to those who fear You, and good hope to those who seek You." We thereby express the wish that the shadows that still darken Israel's position may vanish, and that hostility directed against Israel may soon come to an end.

But must we not include other wishes in our plea? First and foremost we must pray that our religious life may flourish, even while storms rage in the outside world. Let us gain greater knowledge and appreciation for the faith of our ancestors. Let us strive to an ever higher degree to understand Judaism's purity and uplifting quality, and demonstrate our joyful participation in Jewish religious life. May our families and our homes become solemn locales for the cultivation of religious feelings, and may we imbue our youth with our ancestors' beliefs and energize them to an extent greater than what we see these days. May all the members of our congregation look to the house of God for edification and inner strengthening, their hearts drawn here whether moved by joy or depressed by sorrow. May peace and harmony ever dwell in our midst, so that no breach or discord will ever tear us asunder.

May such be our yearnings as we present our prayers before God's throne. Then will our festival cast its luminous rays of light on our future lives, to ennoble and sanctify us. As we wish, from the depth of our hearts, all goodness for ourselves as well as for our entire religious community and for all of humanity, we will see the realization of our efforts in happiness and blessing. So may God grant. Amen.

SACRIFICES

Second Day Rosh Hashanah 5659 [1898]

When, at the start of this new year, our thoughts turn backward to the past, we cannot but conclude that such reminiscence has in some measure enhanced our inner lives. As we ponder over what has remained of the past, and what purpose and goals we see in our future, we are led to introspection and to an awareness of our limitations. The gain for the individual from this thought process is inestimable. Indeed, each Rosh Hashanah has an urgent, uplifting, civilizing, and sanctifying effect on all of us. The great multitudes that are everywhere crowding houses of God on this day, inspired by a festive mood, bear witness that the Jewish heart is not impervious to the religious sounds with which our New Year festival calls us.

How abundantly appropriate are our festival prayers in directing our thoughts toward a higher level of sanctity, whose ennobling influence will not diminish even when, in the next few days, the sounds of our prayers will no longer be heard. You will no doubt be able to experience this yourselves when you contemplate your prayers, and immerse yourselves in the richness of their content, listening to their exhortations and allowing their gentle yet urgent messages to speak to your hearts.

I wish, today, to draw your attention to the portion of the Torah which we have just read, and which is so ideally suited to evoke in us ennobling thoughts about the New Year. Our Torah reading describes the binding of Isaac, recording both the trial of Abraham, as God asks him to give up his only son, as well as Isaac's submission to this Divine command. What a magnificent example, also for us, to direct our thoughts to God, especially at this time of the year, when a new chapter in our lives opens up before us. The sacrifices of old we no longer have. We rather adhere to the principle enunciated by the prophet Samuel to King Saul: "To obey is better than a choice offering, to be attentive better than the fat of rams" (I Samuel 15:22). And yet, obedience to God's commandments is also a sacrifice, at times much more difficult than the bringing of burnt offerings. In that sense, we, too, are required today to make sacrifices, though different in form from what our ancestors brought.

Abraham was willing to offer up his only son, the one who was promised to him, the one on whom all his hopes for the future rested. An onerous task it was indeed, a testimony to his subordination to and unreserved trust in the Divine plan that made this action necessary. How otherwise would God permit such a demand to be issued? Such readiness could only have been the product of Abraham's earlier life. Early on, the carrying out of God's command to leave his native land and the house of his parents constituted a great sacrifice, and sacrifice he did throughout his life, as God tested him on ten occasions. With these traits of self-conquest and self-sacrifice in behalf of our God, Abraham will ever be our role model. Life demands of us constant sacrifices, which no one, be he prince or beggar, can completely escape. If we do not bring them willingly, they are often wrested from us.

From his earliest years, a child must accustom himself to sacrifice rather than follow his heart's unbridled impulses. Father, mother, educator, and teacher are at his side, always erecting altars upon which he must sacrifice, be it for the sake of his health, his training, or his good breeding. As the years rush along, the sacrifices increase. Freedom and innocence must be sacrificed on the school's altar. In formulating our lives along certain plans, parts of the present must yield in order to secure the future. Were it not for sacrifice we would have to shun human society and withdraw into solitude. Progress without sacrifice is impossible. Even when we have reached maturity and established our own households, the spirit of sacrifice can never abate. Our professions, providing for our family, our role as father and husband – all these demand sacrifice. Only with our dying breath do we cease to sacrifice.

Sadly, not all of our sacrifices are dedicated to high and noble goals, nor is all of our readiness to self-sacrifice a blessing. How often do we see offerings of folly that resemble the dreadful gifts dedicated, in ancient days, to the Molech. We seek pleasure but are never satisfied; we worship the god of wealth, surrendering the innocence of our hearts and the nobility of our good name.

To the gods of fashion and of passion we offer disastrous sacrifices, sometimes at the cost of domestic happiness and family prosperity.

What guards us today from bringing such offerings, which compromise our human dignity and rob us of happiness and peace of mind? It is the very same that protected ancient Israel from the gruesome pagan sacrifices of those times: building altars to our religion and dedicating ourselves to the glory of God.

Indeed, my dear listeners, one must readily admit that the sacrifices that Judaism requires of us are considerable: self-denial while watching others devote themselves to pleasures, and self-control where others show no restraint. Our religion has erected, on many sides, fences that make us pause and deliberate on our actions. Where our religion has allowed us more latitude, our adversaries eagerly erect obstacles that make our voluntary sacrifices even more onerous.

And yet there is one aspect of our religious sacrifices to which we can point with much pride, something that compensates us amply for any deprivation that might be demanded of us. At no time does our religion require of us sacrifices that defy common sense or understanding, or that are unreasonably stringent – nothing that shuns the penetrating light of understanding. It rather requires sacrifices which, while curbing our pleasures, allow us the inner freedom to direct our earthly impulses to the ennobling of man and to what the Almighty demands of us, sacrifices that make us worthy of our history and our past. Any deprivation demanded by such sacrifices is repaid to us, manifold, in happiness, in ennoblement, and in strength of character.

My listeners: While all peoples in ancient times brought sacrifices, Israel, from time immemorial, has been a people of sacrifice and of sacrificing. As long as the Temple in Jerusalem was in existence, daily offerings, mornings and evenings, were made to the Eternal. However, it was when the Temple stood in ruins that the time of real sacrifice began. What Abraham intended to carry out on Mount Moriah's heights – and was spared him by Heavenly grace – was in later times literally carried out by thousands of our forefathers who refused to sever the religious bond that united them with their children. Here it is not in the figurative sense that we are speaking. Under the horrible conditions of medieval persecutions, loving fathers, by their own hands, would subject themselves and their families to death rather than renounce the faith of their ancestors. And even when all earthly support failed them and the world about them was sinking, they would yet intone, with solemn fervor, the words of our daily prayers: אשרינו מה טוב חלקנו ומה נעים גורלנו – "We are fortunate! How goodly is our portion, how pleasant our lot" (from the daily morning prayer).

Times have fortunately become more favorable and quiet, but, alas, our spirit of sacrifice is not what it was, having lost much of its alacrity and vigor. Parents nowadays are unwilling to impose on their children those sacrifices that will preserve their faith, and they even question whether they should really accustom their children to give of themselves for the sake of our belief. But, you parents, rest assured: if you will not accustom your children to sacrifice on the altar of our religion, they will one day bring offerings on other altars, whose incense will not be sweet smelling either to you or to God.

Let us therefore hold up as a shining model Abraham's spirit of sacrifice and Isaac's devotion, and let the exalted example of these heroes serve to uplift us and strengthen us in our belief. Let us resolve to place ourselves, with our entire being, in the service of the Eternal, to take to heart His teachings and to follow in His commands. Then will this Rosh Hashanah festival have given us renewed strength, as we embark on our journey into a new year. Amen.

THE WAYS OF GOD

Kol Nidrei 5658 [1897]

My devout listeners: If we regard the millions of our coreligionists the world over, wherever those acknowledging the one and only God have pitched their tents, who have gathered, at this very moment, to pray in houses of worship, in numbers and with devotion never seen in the course of the year, we experience an uplifting feeling of pride. We see that our profession of faith manifests its beneficent influence and captivating power even in this, our reputedly irreligious generation.

We are living in a period when the granite structure of our religion is in greater danger than ever before, partly due to assault from without, partly due to indifference from within. The watchman standing guard in God's vineyard often asks, what form will the future take? Not that he is concerned about the continuity of our religion, since only what is mortal can fade away; what is of Divine origin is by its nature indissoluble and eternally secure, whether guaranteed by the multitudes or defended by a miniscule group of champions. It is rather the people that worry the watchman. Can their inner lives be uplifted so that they remain ethical and do not lose their way in life's confusion, or will they drown in the tidal wave of mundane human existence?

With the arrival of our festival today, all apprehension must disappear. We realize that the sun of our belief has not lost its vitality, nor have our hearts lost their warm receptiveness. Under the sheet of ice with which the bitter assaults of life have surrounded our hearts, there remain our religious feelings, our love, and our attachment to the beliefs of our ancestors.

There is something exalted and uplifting in this festival: an indescribable feeling capturing Israel's heart and soul. Sounds from a distant and holy world reverberate, seizing us with the feeling of God's omnipotence, and lifting us up with magical force beyond our commonplace endeavors. What is earthly has lost its attraction, its luster stripped of its deception. The soul is seized with eager anticipation of a more perfect world. And just as in former times the prophets enthusiastically answered God's call, though mindful that persecution and sacrifice awaited them, so do we joyfully heed God's call, and willingly submit to the self-denial awaiting us as we consecrate ourselves to the service of God. קול קורא, "A Heavenly voice is calling," and what message is this voice sending us? It is the same message that the ancient prophet heard:

קול קורא במדבר פנו דרך ה' ישרו בערבה מסלה לא-להינו – "A voice calls out: 'Clear the way of the Lord in the wilderness; make a straight path in the desert, a road for our God.'"

כל גיא ינשה וכל הר וגבעה ישפלו והיה העקב למישור והרכסים לבקעה – "Every valley will be raised, and every mountain and hill will be lowered; the crooked will become straight and the heights will become valley."

ונגלה כבוד ה' וראו כל בשר יחדו כי פי ה' דבר – "The glory of the Lord will be revealed, and all flesh together will see that the mouth of the Lord has spoken." (Isaiah 40:3–5)

These verses express the spirit of what has led us today into these sacred halls, and they articulate our aspirations. We are to smooth the way for the Lord and clear His path, so that the glory of God become manifest and all recognize that the Eternal is speaking to us.

Let us then, my devout listeners, learn how we can reach this goal.

במדבר פנו דרך ה' ישרו בערבה מסלה לא-להינו – "Clear the way of the Lord in the wilderness; make a straight path in the desert, a road for our God." This phrase may well sound strange to us. Are we, feeble human beings, asked to clear a path for the mighty Creator of this world? His indelible footprints radiate to the farthest corners of the universe, and His seal is imprinted on all living things. Are not the orbits of the glittering stars in the firmament His path? Were they not created with the wink of an eye and do they not bear witness to His wisdom? The eagle, circling in the highest regions of the atmosphere, or the worm, winding his way through the dust – they also smooth a path for His will. Everything is humbled before His will and his mysterious guidance. No obstacles impede His strength, nor are there barriers in the consummation of Divine might. And unbeknownst to us, we humans, like it or not, also fit into the framework of God's rule and are vital parts in that incessantly working process whereby God manifests His intentions.

And yet, there is another world where God's intent holds sway, where, strange to say, the roads of God may be blocked, where obstacles of all sorts block the carrying out of His will. You might traverse and explore the entire universe, ascend to immeasurable heights – everywhere you will find the hand of God, if you will but look. It is only in the human heart and in man's consciousness where you might find a wasteland so desolate that the search for God would be in vain. It is here that man's noblest aspirations may result in the most profound humiliation, and the magnificent gift of free will becomes a barrier to approaching the Creator. It is in our hearts and souls that we must pave and clear the way for God, because crookedness promotes cunning rather than wisdom. Bleak, sterile heights of spiteful pride must be lowered, and stifling plains of indifference raised. Barren deserts and bare plains have to be rebuilt and replanted.

To be sure, the human breast is endowed with Divine vitality. The psalmist finds the most eloquent testimony of God's authority in the babble of infants and children (Psalms 8:3). When, however, the human heart becomes the arena of human lust, and when dark forces hold dominion over us, threatening to drag us into the puddles of sin, then all traces of the godly and the eternal disappear from within us, and our heart becomes a wilderness, sprouting forth only poisonous weeds. Degeneration of spiritual life follows, and we lose our receptiveness to God's rule.

May this day halt the course of our backsliding and return us closer to God. May this festival of Yom Kippur bring fruition to our noble and sacred striving toward perfection. Like a messenger of God with blissful tidings does this festival approach, singing שלום שלום לרחוק ולקרוב, "Peace, peace to him that is far off, and to him that is near" (Isaiah 57:19). May the splendor of God be revealed therein. May it appear to us as the "Sabbath of Sabbaths." When the exalted, Almighty God, at Whose blink of an eye the world was formed and Who, with one breath, can bring down from their lofty heights the high and mighty here on earth, when this God lovingly descends to us like a father would, drawing His children nigh to Him, showing forbearance for our weakness and indulgence for our faults – then what happier message can the human heart experience, and what more sublime tidings would the soul want to hear?

This incomparable message should arouse a meaningful echo within us, serving as a motive to bring us closer to the Eternal. If God draws nigh unto you, would you possibly want to distance yourself from Him? If the all-loving God bestows His love on you, could you possibly refuse? He opens the gates leading to Him; would you decline to enter? He desires to live in our hearts; shall we not smooth the path and pave the road to His entrance? O, rid yourself of the pride that leads to arrogance and prevents you from recognizing your own limitations. Bow down in pious recognition of the all-conquering power of love that radiates upon you from God's shining grace. Open your hearts and ears to the wondrous voices of forgiveness and salvation beckoning you to God's proximity, to liberate you from the burden of guilt which your self-deception has brought on. Consider what godly demands were placed before you and which of them you really carried out. Consider the gap between what you have done and what you really could have done, had you been less self-seeking and less stubborn. Are you aware of how far you have distanced yourself from the paths on which your ancestors walked, paths that did not have so much external glitter as inner satisfaction?

When you have considered all this, you will delight in the eternal Lord, as tomorrow's Haftarah indicates. He walks you to the heights of the earth where the goodness of God dwarfs all earthly matters, and where God allows you, once again, to enjoy the heritage of your ancestor Jacob (Isaiah 58:14). You will renew your bond with your forefathers' beliefs, inspired by what is holy for Israel and must ever remain holy. Tie around yourself the band that joins all of us in humble worship of God, the bond that unites us with our Jewish brethren as well as with all of humanity.

Let us then, my dear listeners, utilize this period of grace that has been granted to us, and make proper use of this Heaven-sent gift. The gates of Heaven are open to receive our prayers. In our spiritual gaze, we see God's ladder, angels ascending and descending, offering our humble homage and pious feelings before the Heavenly throne, and bringing atonement down to us. Let us then ready ourselves for this holy work, and take courage from the declaration of our forefathers: חזק ונתחזק בעד עמנו ובעד ערי א-להינו וה' יעשה הטוב בעיניו, "Be strong, and let us both be strong, for the sake of our people and for the sake of the cities of our God, and the Lord will do what is good in His eyes" (II Samuel 10:12). Amen.

Our Collective Responsibility

Kol Nidrei 5660 [1899]

He who wishes to understand the feelings of Israel's collective soul in its most tender state, and capture the very innate, primordial sentiments of our religious community, let him enter this evening into our midst. Our lives in the outside world surge along in their customary track, pressing, rushing, battling, and struggling. Time is regarded as a precious commodity, as we divide up each day in the most economic manner and painstakingly utilize each hour. And this Sturm und Drang, which has cast its special imprint on our times, is also reflected in the lives of people. This haste and unrest, this persistent tension and incessant striving for progress filling our psyche is all the product of our own making. The family head does not allot for himself the time he really needs to devote to his household. Only rarely does he concern himself with matters other than those which have a monetary value.

We do not sufficiently contemplate the fact that our life on this earth must one day come to an end, that the most secured position in life, the most extensive sphere of influence, and the most successful of businesses will one day be wrenched away from us. The charm and worth of all that delights and uplifts will one day be lost to us.

So it goes in our daily lives. We tend to ignore the message of the Sabbaths and festivals that bid us to call a "halt" to our daily race and gain circumspection and inner composure. Amidst the tumult of everyday life, this voice is often muffled and its message irrelevant. We tend, rather, to heed those messages that make much noise, that translate into numbers and figures, and that seem to have a practical use.

We observe this phenomenon in our day, not only in the camps of Israel but in all circles and in all strata of society. The pursuit of the material and the preoccupation with the pleasures of the times have taken over all classes of society, poor and rich. There is, to be sure, an appreciation for the ideal; life is not all dull and empty. And yet, the pursuit of the ideal has lost its purity, as we look to make our lives more cheerful rather than to ennoble them.

And now, my dear listeners, from this frenzied way of life, which Israel shares with members of other religions, we Jews have withdrawn this evening, shutting out all of the demands of the outside world, renouncing the transient fashions of the day, so that we may dedicate ourselves to what is holy and noble. We see here, anew, the soul of the Jewish people, emerging in all of its radiant serenity, cleansed of all impurity. Today's festival reveals the essence of our Jewish way of thinking. As we rededicate ourselves to God and seek atonement from Him, it is the manner in which we acknowledge our sins and beg for forgiveness that brings out so clearly the nature of Jewish spiritual life.

The prevailing theme of our prayers, from the start of our festival until tomorrow evening, derives from our confession of חטאנו, "We have sinned." This idea recurs in the manifold expressions of our liturgy, as we enumerate all conceivable instances in which we have transgressed, so that our hearts may be immersed in contrition and the path to repentance be cleared. This is, in and of itself, quite remarkable. But no less significant is the fact that our prayers to God are recited in the plural form; that is, we enumerate our sins collectively. It is the manner in which we confess our sins that deserves a closer consideration and to which I want to devote tonight's message.

My dear listeners, among the sins that we enumerate in our confession on this day, there are, no doubt, some that we did not commit. To be sure, we did blunder and transgress, partly out of thoughtlessness, partly out of neglect of our moral and religious commandments. Yet in every series of enumerated transgressions many will find sins that they never, in their entire life, committed. Nevertheless, our religion bids us confess these sins so that we may feel ourselves as part of a totality, a totality in which there are some who are virtuous and others who transgress. Some might want to reject this kind of responsibility, and wonder why all of Israel must make amends for the transgressions of but a few.

There is yet another reason why, on this day, we charge ourselves with sins that we did not commit. Are we to feel responsible for our deeds alone, and not for the consequences they may have on society? Before the tribunal of the law of the land, that might well be the case, but never in the arena of our moral conscience, never before the Heavenly court.

Our sages have left us an instructive parable: A ship once embarked upon the high seas filled with passengers, each of whom had an assigned place for the duration of the journey. One of the passengers began to drill a hole in the side of the ship next to his assigned place, and water started to gush in. "Miserable fellow, what are you doing?" cried the captain of the ship, to which he calmly replied, "תחתי אני קודח – This is my place, which I rented. Why can I not do as I please, since I am drilling only in my assigned place?" "But you are hurling us all into destruction," countered the frightened fellow travelers, "because the entire ship will sink on your account"(*Yalkut Shimoni Iyov* 920).

My listeners: "By what right," some people might claim, "can I be held accountable for my ethical and religious actions? What I do, I do for myself, and just as I do not attend to the affairs of others, I wish to remain unencumbered in my doings. תחתי אני קודח and if I transgress, nobody needs to answer for me or to do penance for me."

Oh, desist, you most inconsiderate individual! You are mistaken if you think that you belong to yourself only. Do you not realize that you might be setting an example for others, that unthinking people may become influenced by your actions? You are drilling only in your own ground, but is it not also the ground of your religious community, the ground of human society? Will you allow the ravaging deluge of the denial of our faith to inundate other people's pastures? Our spiritual life represents the sum total of what was achieved over the millennia, and we are therefore bound to those who came before us as well as those who succeed us. In our time, as well, we are linked by thousands of bonds to all living people. We are subject, together with them, to the laws of reciprocal action; we are influenced by them, and they by us.

It is for this reason that our sages regarded the violation of a religious statute in public as a far greater transgression than when the same is done in secret. Morally the two are, of course, the same. But in reference to its destructive influence, there is an enormous difference between what takes place in secret and what transpires in public. And just as a stone thrown into the water causes increasingly wider circles of ripples, setting parts of the water far removed from the original site of impact into motion, so do our actions evoke spreading undulations in the souls of those close to us. We may not see this with our eyes, but it is there, nevertheless.

In ancient Israel when a murdered human being was found lying in an open field and it was not known who committed that murder, the elders of the town closest to the scene of the crime were commanded by our Torah to perform an act of atonement and make a confession: ידינו לא שפכו את הדם הזה ועינינו לא ראו, "Our hands did not spill this blood nor did our eyes see it" (Deuteronomy 21:7). "Would one imagine," asks the Talmud, "that the elders and most respected of the people be suspected of having committed such a crime? "No," reads the interpretation, "they were but to acknowledge that this occurrence was not caused indirectly by their action nor by their omission, and that, to the extent possible, they provided adequate security in their midst; and, on the other hand, that they provided the necessary support for the needy, so that no one should have been driven by extreme need to commit murder" (Talmud Bavli, *Sotah* 45b).

My dear listeners: We do not reflect enough, these days, on what share the totality has in the ruin of the individual. In searching for its cause, we must look beyond the site of the offense. "We must not perceive the defects in society solely where they give vent to crime, but rather in their relationship with cause and effect" (Kalthoff, *An der Wende des Jahrhunderts*). Or, to express it pictorially: rather than watching the thunder and lightning, pay attention to the harmful vapors rising to form a thunderstorm, while menacing clouds conglomerate.

If we consider this advice, no one in today's society can feel entirely innocent of a crime committed in some other place. Do you know with certainty that you might not have given the first impetus to one who now totally disregards all godly and human demands and makes light of what is holy and sacrosanct, or whether an evil act on your part, such as a frivolous word or the deprecation of religious and moral ideals, might perhaps have caused someone who was already foundering to sink yet deeper? The disparagement of anything religious on the part of individuals can cause a religious and even moral decline among those who are already on spiritually shaky ground, because your bad example undermines what little support he still has. And if we seek to uncover the motives that led an individual to criminal action, some might well become frightened on recognizing the share they might have had in causing the ruin of an individual, and shudder at the responsibility they must bear for their thoughtless act.

It is for that reason that we confess today sins for which we know we do not have any direct responsibility. If this leads us to scrutinize more closely our own personal conduct, our future actions on behalf of the community will be all the more beneficial, and our lives ennobled and more dedicated to God.

Let us then, my listeners, utilize in full measure this day, which God appointed as a day of mercy. Let us examine rigorously and with great sincerity our actions and conduct, and bring improvement where we erred. Then will the barrier between us and our God, which our sins have erected, recede, so that we will once again be at one with our Creator. And when, at the conclusion of our festival, tomorrow's sun will set, and night will cover the earth with its dark wings, we will sense in our hearts the call emanating from on high: סלחתי, "I have forgiven." Amen.

SEEKING GOD

Mussaf of Yom Kippur 5661 [1900]

שמע ה׳ קולי אקרא וחנני וענני. לך אמר לבי בקשו פני, את פניך ה׳ אבקש.
Hear, O Lord, when I call with my voice, and be gracious unto me, and answer me. To You my heart speaks: Seek my face; Your face, O Lord, will I seek. (Psalms 27:7–8)

It is several weeks now that we have been reciting these words, morning and evening at the end of our services. We began with the first day of the month of Elul, as we ushered in the yearly time of penitence for the Jewish people. It is today, however, that we first sense the full meaning of these words. We have withdrawn from the clamorous outside world, and taken refuge here in proximity to God, totally dedicating ourselves to Him, seeking His countenance in fervent prayer, that He may look down favorably upon us with forgiveness.

We have today broken away from what was until now holding us captive. The temptations and hypocrisy of the world have no influence on us here today. We only hear the soft tones of our religion speaking to our feelings, their gentle admonishing voices addressing our hearts. We hear in these voices, with much greater clarity than the shrill sounds of the outer world, what our true needs are.

Our religion is acclaiming the arrival of that God-given day of mercy, announcing that the gates of heaven are today opened wider than usual. The sun of Divine forgiveness is shining on us benevolently, like a kindly father gently pressing his sinful but remorseful child to his breast. He has given us this day so that we, by means of contrition, remorse, and self-improvement, might seek His pardon.

We have eagerly followed these instructions and have come here today to seek God's countenance, knowing well that we may at times have forgotten Him. Not wishing to be shaken out of our indolence – or shall we rather call it lack of consideration – we may even have dismissed God from our minds. We did not heed His warnings, stubbornly following the paths of sin and perversity, of conceit and of arrogance – and all those other evil forces that lodge in our inner being and make us subservient to them. And yet, reminders of the Almighty God, Who controls our lives and our destiny, are everywhere: be it the dark rain clouds across the skies, the dazzling lightning convulsing down through the atmosphere, or the sun smiling in the blue firmament. Indeed, everything the eye perceives points to the Almighty, Who guides us along our path of life and guards us from sinking into the abyss.

And precisely because we turned a deaf ear to that majestic and mighty voice of God calling to us, have we come today to the house of God to hear that quiet voice of our religion. But have we thereby fulfilled our religious requirement, and have we indeed found God? My devout listeners, the Book of God instructs us, by means of the words of the prophet Zephaniah, in what manner we are to search for God: בקשו את ה׳...בקשו צדק, בקשו ענוה "Seek the Lord…seek righteousness, seek humility" (Zephaniah 2:3). Let us this day learn a lesson from this declaration.

I.

בקשו את ה׳ – "Seek the Lord" is the call of the prophet's voice, and we hear in our hearts its meaningful echo: את פניך ה׳ אבקש, "Your countenance will I seek." Hence we have come here to search for God by means of prayer, while denying ourselves all corporeal needs in favor of our more lofty spiritual needs. Let not our thoughts drift to our work, our business, or what we must accomplish tomorrow. Only if our prayers are sincere and represent the outpouring of the innermost of our hearts will our spirits be enabled to seek God's presence.

However, this festival and the prophet's admonition ask of us much more than just to seek God in our prayers. We Jews are members of a community that, though scattered throughout the world, looks back at a past extending thousands of years. Over the millennia, our forefathers stood in solemn contrition before God on this day, and thus for all time, extending even to our present generation. In celebrating Yom Kippur our forefathers drew unforgettable strength and enthusiasm for their Divine purpose of propagating the faith here on earth. On יום הכפורים, they always found their way back to God, even when they were in danger of being led astray. This day served as a fountain of youth into which the soul could be immersed, emerging rejuvenated and invigorated in its service to God.

This places on us the sacred duty to align ourselves, as noble members, with the preceding generations. We, for our part, must ensure that Israel will not shirk its God-given duty to preserve for future generations that for which our forefathers fought and suffered: our sacred God-given religion and our Torah.

And especially on this Yom Kippur, a day totally devoted to God, we are to render an account of ourselves and ask whether we have succeeded in our mission as human beings and as Jews. Tell me then, you men and women, boys and girls, have you at all times maintained a full awareness of your Jewishness? All too often it is evil circumstances that remind us of our being Jews. But is this really the only thing that reminds you of your roots and your religion? Would you not rather cherish that which is yours by birth and by heritage? Our forefathers held tight to their faith in spite of countless martyrdoms and persecutions. They did not forsake their God even when they lost everything and were driven from one place to another. We today are not asked to make such sacrifices. But should that mean a weakening in our love and devotion? What matters more than just acknowledging membership in the Jewish community is enthusiastic participation. What matters is that we fulfill the commandments of our religion, uphold its precepts, and follow its instructions, both in our personal conduct and in the building of our family life. What matters is that we sanctify and celebrate the Sabbath, the jewel of our religion, heed the message of our festivals, and seek to honor and worship God in His house.

Our pride and fortune as Jews rests on our espousal of that faith which was given to us at Sinai and which was humanity's first lesson in morality. Let us demonstrate that we are Jews not just in name but in conviction, showing the very same enthusiasm that our forefathers had for what will always remain our heritage, lest we sink beneath the shaky ground on which we stand.

May today's festival motivate us in this direction. Let us solemnly resolve on this holy day to conduct our lives in the light of this day of mercy. We will then not only have sought God, we will have found Him!

II.

My devout listeners: When the sun sets on this day and our Yom Kippur celebration will have drawn us back, in thought and feeling, to our God, we will once again step into the outer world to our daily pursuits. It is then that we must heed the second message of the prophet, "Seek righteousness and humility," so that this day will not have passed us by without leaving its imprint on us. To think that the worship of God in His house is sufficient to discharge one's duty would be a gross misunderstanding of our religion. And yet, the type of service which we dedicate to our Creator outside of the synagogue may be associated with much temptation. We are in danger of sinning against Him and of distancing ourselves from His presence. Our actions must be marked by fairness and honesty, never to deviate from the path of truth even by a hairsbreadth; not to stray from the ways of virtue even when temptation promises much; not to be seduced by the expectation of profit to bend the truth and commit wrong; not to give in to hatred, but rather to act with conciliation and to forgive willingly; to avoid envy and slander – these are the true ways of seeking God.

"Proceed with humility and modesty!" My dear listeners, here we might sometimes be found guilty of behaving with arrogance and insolence. It does not seem appropriate, on this day when we confess and express regret for our sins, that we should be silent in the face of admonition brought before us. We should rather ask ourselves honestly: Did we not in some way contribute to bringing upon us this unkind judgment? We therefore must admit that we may be hard-hearted, abusive, and disparaging of others and yet not recognize these faults in ourselves.

Let us therefore walk humbly in our ways and not intrude where we are not wanted. Let us not call attention to ourselves by noisy, unruly behavior or by making ourselves conspicuous in showy pomp and boastfulness. We should rather live our lives in a manner that will shed honor upon us, working humbly for the common good and with love for our fellow man.

Our sages tell us that when Solomon erected the Temple on Mount Moriah he structured the windows so that they were narrow on the inside and wide on the outside (*Rashi*, I Kings 6:4), suggesting that far more than the sun's rays can illuminate, the radiation of God's light from inside the Temple will illuminate and warm the outer world. If on this God-appointed day of mercy we seek Him out, then the light which has been kindled in our hearts today will radiate from our lives and illuminate our path through life, free from all stumbling blocks.

My devout listeners: Prior to our returning to the tumultuous and noisy outer world, we are being called here by the voices of our dearly departed. Our hearts are full of sorrow and emotion as we remember them and as we now direct our fervent prayers in their behalf to our Creator. These transfigured souls are, no doubt, gazing down upon us from their lofty heights, while our prayers bring them merit before the Divine throne. As a result of our prayers, that invisible bond tying us, beyond the grave, to them becomes stronger and more intimate. May our remembrance of our dearly departed strengthen us in our dedication to God and firm our resolve to live our lives in accordance with the solemnity of this day. Then will we demonstrate that we sought God, and that we found Him. Amen.

The Effect of Our Celebration

Ne'ilah 5661 [1900]

כי כאשר ירד הגשם והשלג מן השמים ושמה לא ישוב, כי אם הרוה את הארץ והולידה והצמיחה, ונתן זרע לזרע ולחם לאכל, כן יהיה דברי אשר יצא מפי, לא ישוב אלי ריקם כי אם עשה את אשר חפצתי והצליח אשר שלחתיו – "For just as the rain and snow descend from heaven and will not return there, but water the earth and cause it to produce and sprout, and give seed to him who sows and food to him who eats, so shall be My word that issues from My mouth; it will not return to Me unfulfilled but it shall accomplish that which I desired and bring success whereto I sent it."

כי בשמחה תצאו ובשלום תובלון, ההרים והגבעות יפצחו לפניכם רנה וכל עצי השדה ימחאו כף – "For in joy shall you go out, and in peace shall you be led forth. The mountains and hills will break out in glad song before you, and all the trees of the field will clap their hands."

תחת הנעצוץ יעלה ברוש ותחת הסרפד יעלה הדס, והיה לה׳ לשם לאות עולם לא יכרת – "In place of the thorn bush a cypress will rise, and in place of the nettle a myrtle will rise; this will be a monument to the Lord, an eternal sign never to be cut off" (Isaiah 55:10–13).

My dear listeners: Action and consequence, sincere repentance, and a contrite return to God – all of these define our Yom Kippur service, and the prophet describes these sentiments so admirably. As the rain and the snow descend, making the earth fruitful and causing it to sprout, so has the word of the Eternal descended upon us today. Our hearts are impregnated with fertile germs for the future. The spiritual rain has benevolently fallen upon all of us in equal measure. Here, in this house of God, we are like one, having the same aspirations, sharing the same sentiments. Some of you might have come here today without a clear sense or expectation of what this day would hold in store for you. Others might be here because that has been your custom since childhood, or because reverence so dictated. The mere fact that you have come, entered the sphere of the holy, joined with the general community, a congregation ardently devout and contrite, casting their glance inward with remorse and heavenward in prayer – you have thereby achieved full membership.

כל הנגע במזבח יקדש – "Whatever touches the altar of the Eternal becomes sanctified" (Exodus 29:37). The collective devotion, which blazes heavenward like the holy sacrificial flame, kindles in each individual a spark of godly sentiments. Illuminated by the sun of this day of mercy and moistened by the dew of God's auspicious word, even the least receptive heart will respond to the holiness of this day. Its message is so rich in joy and blessing that it cannot but affect us all. And when our Father in Heaven beckons us, who can ignore His call? More lovingly than a mother speaks to her child or a father admonishes his son does God speak to us through the medium of the prophet.

שובו בנים שובבים ארפה משובתיכם – "Return unto Me, you wayward children, and I will heal your waywardness" (Jeremiah 3:22). And though you are wanting and have sinned against Me, I am your loving Father, and you, My cherished children.

כי לא לעולם אריב ולא לנצח אקצוף – "For not forever will I contend, nor will I always be angry" (Isaiah 57:16). And should we still remain hesitant, God would encourage us into firm resolve, calling on the prophet Malachi to sound the message: שובו אלי ואשובה אליכם, "Return to Me and I will return to you" (Malachi 3:7). As a father lovingly embraces his estranged son, who has returned to him contrite and mindful of his past mistakes, so will I accept you and lighten the burden of your contrition and your return. Readily do I forgive your offense.

ונסלח לכל עדת בני ישראל ולגר הגר בתוכם כי לכל העם בשגגה – "And the entire assembly of Israel shall be forgiven, and the stranger dwelling in their midst, for the entire people sinned unintentionally" (Numbers 15:26). You have failed to recognize my Fatherly goodness because you did not understand my ways.

My dear listeners: Such heavenly voices reverberating to us on this Yom Kippur cannot but make an impression on us. With love and understanding let us take them to heart. And just as the rain and the snow descend from the heavens, and do not return until they have watered the earth and made it fruitful, so will the promises emanating from God's mouth not return unfulfilled. They will have achieved their desired effect and accomplished the purpose of their mission.

"In place of the thorn bush a cypress will rise, and in place of the nettle a myrtle will rise." Similarly, our hearts, previously empty, are today receptive to what is godly. Even those of us who are indifferent can today feel the spiritual joy of what is eternal. We realize that our noble religion, implanted as a tender twig in the hearts of our forefathers thousands of years ago, has not lost its freshness in spite of the intensely blazing sun of our modern times, but rather continues to blossom and sprout its refreshing fruits.

The teachings of the one and only, benevolent, perfect God of all, who calls humanity His children, whose teachings lend us our human dignity, a dignity which though sometimes tarnished will never be lost – the teachings that in spite of our lapses and our guilt, we can receive atonement and forgiveness directly from God, without the help of any intermediary, if we but show sincere regret and penitence and resolve to improve our lives – these teachings have today permeated our consciousness and our hearts, as we come to realize that our Judaism is priceless beyond all earthly possession.

This day of Yom Kippur affects us all. Our hearts beat with greater sanctity and our souls with more sincere emotion toward God. In holy fervor we have broken down the wall that we erected, separating us from God, and have found our way back to Him. Despite our waning physical strength, we experience this newly attained partnership with almost heavenly bliss. We have achieved atonement, and our trust in God's help has been restored. We feel that God has forgiven us for our sins. A beautiful sensation is coursing through our very being: the awareness that we have today achieved the ultimate victory – the victory over ourselves, the victory over our earthly inclinations, a victory to cherish what was always holy for our forefathers and what must for us remain holy always.

כי בשמחה תצאו ובשלום תובלון, "For in joy shall you go out, and in peace shall you be led forth" – with benevolent joy, the joy that offers a pure, innocent lifestyle, the joy of realizing that the godly in you has today celebrated a tremendous triumph in having once again become cognizant of the lofty demands made of our lives, the joy for that which is eternal and everlasting in our short-lived existence, and for the mission and destiny of Israel. ובשלום תובלון, "And in peace shall you be led forth" – true, undisturbed peace of mind. This peace has been offered you today, but its preservation requires that you, henceforth, renew it each and every day so that it will not succumb to the pressures of everyday life. We must preserve our beautiful feeling of being at one with our God by preserving our connection to Him. Let us hasten to the synagogue more frequently and become active members, rather than allowing our belief to become vague and irrelevant.

"For in joy shall you go out, and in peace shall you be led forth. The mountains and hills will break out in joyful song before you, and all the trees of the field will clap their hands." We appreciate the magnificence of the rays of the sun, the beauty of nature, and the marvel of the creation all the more when we regard it as the work of a benevolent God, a solicitous Creator Who keeps watch over all. Every blade of grass bears witness to His magnitude, every leaf points to His omnipotence, and every small cloud in the sky speaks of His grandeur. We can thus imagine all creatures paying homage to Him, saying, ה׳ אדנינו מה אדיר שמך בכל הארץ, "O Lord, our Master, how mighty is Your name in all the earth" (Psalms 8:10).

"In joy shall you go out, and in peace shall you be led forth" – the joy of having sensed atonement, the peace of being in harmony with God and your faith, and with yourself. If, indeed, this day of Yom Kippur brings this about, והיה לה׳ לשם לאות עולם לא יכרת (Isaiah 55:13), it will be for the glory of the Eternal, and He will ever be your blessing and your salvation. Amen.

The Farewell

Ne'ilah 5662 [1901]

My devoted listeners: If we were to peer into the hearts of the thousands upon thousands of Jews that have, today, dedicated themselves with fervent prayer and solemn devotion to their God – summoning up, at this time of sunset, all those spiritual forces needed to tear down the last barriers to atonement with God – we would then indeed conclude that the flame in the Jewish heart is not extinguished. That flame, first lit amidst thunder and lightning on Mount Sinai, reminds us that, despite some changes in our religious conduct, a rich treasure of holy sentiment remains, making us worthy of our past.

We have today devoted ourselves totally to the Almighty, removed ourselves from all that is mundane, denied ourselves earthly pleasures, and directed our thoughts exclusively to God, so as to enjoy a union with our all-loving Father. And as daylight will soon make way for the night, a chorus of millions will resound in the heavens singing the ancient declaration of our people, שמע ישראל ה׳ א-להינו ה׳ אחד, "Hear, O Israel, the Lord is our God, the Lord is One," for which Jews have fought and with which they went to their deaths. It is our statement that we are all Jews and will be so till our last breath. We thereby demonstrate the folly of those who would seek our destruction. Our devotion to God and to our belief is perhaps greater than that of any other creed on earth.

The stranger might regard our abstention from food and other earthly pleasures as an exceptionally onerous sacrifice. We, however, in our devotion to God, regard such deprivation as negligible in comparison to the internal bliss that this day offers us. Our spiritual elevation more than compensates for any weakness we might experience, and the joy of our reconciliation with our loving Father exceeds any earthly pleasures.

בנעילה מאי אמרי, "At the time of Ne'ilah, what should the congregation proclaim upon hearing the words of the Priestly Blessing?" ask our sages in the Talmud (Talmud Bavli, *Sotah* 40a). They answer that question with the words of Psalms 128:4–6:

הנה כי כן יברך גבר ירא ה׳ – "Behold, for thus shall the man be blessed who fears the Lord."

כל ימי חייך יברכך ה׳ מציון וראה בטוב ירושלים – "The Lord shall bless you out of Zion, and may you see the good of Jerusalem all the days of your life."

וראה בנים לבניך שלום על ישראל – "And see children born unto your children. Peace upon Israel."

Yes, my dear listeners, it is with soulful elation that we feel today that the God-fearing man is blessed. You too will be blessed when tomorrow and in all future days you walk in the ways of God. That certainly does not suggest that your lives be filled with deprivation and self-denial; it would not be in keeping with our belief or with our Divine commandments. We are, rather, bidden to resume our usual duties and obligations. In one sense however we must remain the same: our hearts must unite in the ancient call that accompanies us back into the outer world, that inspiring affirmation of our people: "Hear, O Israel, the Lord is our God, the Lord is One," whereby we declare our unfailing loyalty to God. Indeed, my worthy listeners, today's inspiring celebration will testify that our belief will never wither away. Let the religious fervor that blossomed among us today and on the previous two festivals remain with us continually.

יברכך ה׳ מציון, "The Lord shall bless you out of Zion," וראה בטוב ירושלים כל ימי חייך, "and you shall see the good of Jerusalem all the days of your life." This Zion, this Jerusalem – we see them here not so much as venerable places in the land of our fathers but rather as the fruits of our religious beliefs, central points of our religion. The Lord's blessing shall blossom out of our belief in Him and His timeless teachings, and our worship of God shall bring us strength and fortune all the days of our lives.

וראה בנים לבניך, "And see children born unto your children": behold your grandchildren and rejoice at the sight of them. What a wonderful comfort if your children share with you the enthusiasm for our Jewish ideals. Any parent with a spark of Jewish feeling, through whose arteries courses a drop of Jewish blood, will look at his children and realize that the chord tying us to the millennia of generations is intact. He will realize that he is not the last link in the chain, and that he will implant in his children the holiness that had been transmitted to him. Oh, may you, as you leave this house of God, search for this inner contentment by teaching your children ever to move in God's ways and observe His commandments, thereby guaranteeing Israel's continued existence.

Yes, then we will achieve שלום על ישראל, "Peace upon Israel." Then will Israel be secured against all onslaughts, strengthened by its belief in God and in loyalty to Him. In this final hour, let us dedicate ourselves with fervent devotion to our God, confident that we will be reconciled with Him. We will carry the spiritual joy that we gained here into our everyday lives, and it will sustain us always. May this be God's will. Amen.

THE SUKKAH: A REPRESENTATION OF LIFE

Sukkot 5663 [1902]

Reflection on our lifestyle, remorse and repentance, serene happiness – these are some of the sentiments that our religion causes us to experience yearly during this month of Tishrei as a way of guiding us along the right paths of life. We reflect on the conduct of our lives on Rosh Hashanah, a time when we are most acutely aware of the weakness and frailty of our earthly existence. On Yom Kippur, when our merits – our religious and ethical behavior – are measured in the balance because we have sinned and are found wanting, it is remorse and the hope for repentance that we experience. But now, on this festival of Sukkot, we experience happiness, as the Torah repeatedly commands: ושמחת בחג, "And you shall rejoice in your festival." And והיית אך שמח, "And you shall be truly happy" (Deuteronomy 16:14, 15).

And yet, it is on a basis different from what we would expect that this festival evokes feelings of joy. For this is the season of the ingathering of the produce of the fields. חג הסכת תעשה לך שבעת ימים באספך מגרנך ומיקבך – "You shall make the festival of Sukkot for a seven-day period when you gather in from your threshing floor and from your wine cellar" (Deuteronomy 16:13). The farmer's barn and wine cellars are now filled, and the fields and meadows have tendered their offerings in great abundance. The raw fall weather is beginning, and cold winds are blowing across bare fields. In our well-built houses and comfortably warmed chambers, we are hardly encumbered by the unfriendly season.

How remarkable, then, that the joy of holiday does not find expression within the safety of our homes, but rather, צא מדירת קבע ושב בדירת עראי, "Leave your permanent dwelling and tarry in a precarious hut" (Talmud Bavli, *Sukkah* 2a) is our festival's bidding. The sukkah offers but little protection against the hardships of weather, the cold penetrating its thin walls, and its leafy canopy providing but minimal resistance to wind and rain. But in no way is our joy diminished. We realize that our festival of Sukkot is not just a seven-day holiday of rejoicing but rather a significant lesson in how we are to view our lives and how to find happiness therein. Let us, today, subject these thoughts to closer examination.

I.

Our sages already saw in the sukkah a representation of life. Like the frail sukkah, our lives lack strength and security, despite all supports we attempt to offer. Many dangers pose a threat to our earliest childhood, requiring the totally dedicated care of motherly love to transform that shaky twig of life into a sturdy tree that can withstand the raging storms. Once a mother has succeeded, by means of loving care, in producing a child of her fondest dreams, life's dangers may have diminished, but are never totally eliminated. Oh, how often do we see a robust youth, his life suddenly torn away, or a young girl in the flowering of her bloom, unexpectedly cut off. No, our lives remain uncertain and our future in doubt.

Quite apart from such unexpected events, our existence can become clouded and troublesome when worries rob the spirit of its momentum. Many a hope that the future will be more beautiful has proven delusive. Lovingly cherished expectations remain unfulfilled, while pain and sorrow assault the heart. Indeed, our sages correctly stated that man would be in utter despair were he aware of the many dangers surrounding him. Our festival comes to teach us an apt comparison between the sukkah and the lives we live.

And yet our religion commands us והיית אך שמח, to view life in its happy aspects. Judaism is opposed to regarding life as dismal and gloomy, even if its deficiencies and shortcomings cannot be overlooked. At the pinnacle of our Torah is the verse וירא א-להים את כל אשר עשה והנה טוב מאד, "And God saw all that He had made, and behold it was very good" (Genesis 1:31). This encapsulates our Jewish ideology, and counters the current, popular view of life that our existence is of no worth. Judaism rejects a life of tears and sighs that ultimately leads to despair and self-destruction. Just like the sukkah, life at times seems to offer more shadow than sunlight. And yet, the sukkah's canopy grants us, by day, a view of the sky, the abode of a benevolent Father, and by night a view of the twinkling stars. Thus are our hearts infused with confidence.

II.

While the sukkah bids us view life with serenity, it renders us a message of equal or even greater significance: בסכת תשבו שבעת ימים...למען ידעו דרתיכם כי בסכות הושבתי את בני ישראל בהוציאי אתם מארץ מצרים – "For seven days you shall dwell in booths...so that your generations will know that I caused the Children of Israel to dwell in booths when I took them out of the land of Egypt" (Leviticus 23:42, 43). And were Moses to be speaking to us today, he would rightly say, "So that your descendants will realize that I have, at all times, made the Children of Israel dwell in sukkot." The dwellings of Israel, even into our time, have been meager, mobile huts, erected in one or another location. But do not think that the joy of the festival was in any way diminished by the wretchedness of their lives.

Our sages ask, what were the huts in which Israel lived while in the desert? They answer ענני כבוד היו, "They were clouds of glory" (Talmud Bavli, *Sukkah* 11b). Likewise did a Divine cloud of glory, in later times, protect the houses of Israel.

Let me awaken a memory among you, the older members sitting here. Let your minds drift back to your parents' house and recall those festive hours that you spent there. Your dwellings might have been modest, the light emitted from the oil lamps rather faint. And yet when your pious mothers made preparations and welcomed the Sabbath or the festivals with raised arms, and when Father came home from the house of God, your modest home radiated a heavenly brilliance, and the tumult of life became transformed into peace and tranquility. Did not their spiritual delight greatly exceed the pleasures that we, in our haste and anxiety, experience? Though we might surpass them in earthly pleasures, their spiritual delights well exceeded ours.

The sukkah thus symbolizes this teaching. בסכת תשבו שבעת ימים, "Seven days shall you dwell in booths"; though the house, during this season, offers much greater comforts than the fragile sukkah, it is within those flimsy walls that we are bidden to celebrate this Festival of Joy. Even with less at your disposal, be happy with what you have. Those who have accustomed themselves, early on in life, to live simply and in moderation might have less worry and less unhappiness. Who can estimate the harm that will befall a previously happy family when unreasonable demands are made on life. Modest fortune can be destroyed for those who are not satisfied with their lot but crave greater pleasures.

ושמחת בחגך, "Rejoice in your festival." Seek a life of serene joy, be glad in the goodness that God has bestowed on you, and above all, retain the ability to be happy in your sukkah though your house is bountiful. Practice self-denial amidst abundance and be master over yourself.

If you, dear parents, wish the best for your children, teach them early on to lead a modest life, even when you can afford to give them material pleasures. Who can guarantee that your children will always find themselves in the same circumstances that you now enjoy and will never have to experience deprivation? Do not indulge them in their demands but let them do without excess pleasures. The important lesson that our sukkah teaches is that life, despite its imperfections, has its bright side, which we appreciate all the more when we cast our gaze heavenward. In the midst of plenty, let us be satisfied with less.

When we heed these teachings we can proclaim with the psalmist: כי יצפנני בסכה ביום רעה יסתרני בסתר אהלו בצור ירוממני – "For He will hide me in His shelter on the day of evil, and conceal me in the covert of His tent; He will lift me upon a rock" (Psalms 27:5). Amen.

Bidding the Festivals Farewell

Shemini Atzeret 5663 [1902]

איש כמתנת ידו כברכת ה' א-להיך אשר נתן לך.
Everyone according to his ability to give, according to the blessing that the Lord, your God, has given you. (Deuteronomy 16:17)

These, my dear listeners, are the closing words of the Torah portion we have just read, and could well serve as a summary of our festivals' spiritual message. These festivals, which have been our companions these past several weeks, will now depart from us. Indeed, this day, called עצרת ("concluding festival"), marks the transition from the solemn back to the everyday.

Numerous messages have been directed toward us in rapid succession during the past weeks, and many demands imposed on us will have an impact on how we shape our future lives. Just as a loving father, upon bidding farewell to his departing son, concludes his advice and instruction with the thought that all is intended for his own good and welfare, so does the concluding verse of our Torah reading tell us that all the demands of the preceding festivals should be seen in relation to our ability and our capacity, according to the blessing which God has granted us.

"Everyone according to his ability to give, according to the blessing that the Lord, your God, has given you." Indeed, this applies generally to the commandments, statutes, principles, and instructions that our religion imposes on us. These words can therefore have the dual function of a parting greeting to our holidays, while at the same time serving to lead us toward a more joyful participation in our religion. It is in this sense that we wish to direct our attention more closely on these concluding words.

My dear listeners, though we might conduct our lives with great piety, joyfully worshiping God in the synagogue, we don't always recognize the full extent of our debt to God. Few people are content with the blessings that God has bestowed upon them. Rather than appreciating what we possess, we tend to exaggerate what we lack. Only when we have lost that which in the past we scarcely heeded do we appreciate its full value. With what yearning does the sick person, who always took his well-being for granted, now regard those who are healthy. Many fail to appreciate the God-apportioned gift of simple domestic happiness, seeking rather the diversion and the pleasure outside the confines of their houses and dear ones. And yet when two eyes from which radiated intimate love one day close, and a faithful heart ceases to beat, creating an irreparable break – only then does one realize, too late, what fortune has been lost. Sons and daughters tend to understand only after their parents have departed from this world to what extent they are indebted to them.

In much the same way do we sometimes lack full appreciation of the blessings that God has given us. Our festival therefore bids us consider the parting message of איש כמתנת ידו כברכת ה' א-להיך וגו'. God does grant you His blessing, but it is for us to show Him the appropriate gratitude.

Living in modest circumstances, you may well have some restrictions in your lifestyle and be forced to deny yourself some pleasures that you note others allowing themselves. But is that a reason not to be thankful to God? You have a loving wife, beautiful children, and are able to support them by means of honest work. And should you ever consider the struggle for your existence to be onerous, remember that there are many who would consider themselves most fortunate were they in your position.

And where some might belittle the gifts that God has bestowed upon them, others will ascribe the results of their labors to themselves, not considering the guiding hand of God to Whom they owe their gratitude. Few of us have the attitude of our ancestor Jacob, wretched and poor on his journey from Beersheba to Haran, as he praises God: ונתן לי לחם לאכל ובגד ללבש ושבתי בשלום אל בית אבי והיה ה' לי לא-להים, "And if God will give me bread to eat and clothes to wear, and I return in peace to my father's house, then the Lord will be a God to me" (Genesis 28:20, 21), and upon returning to his fatherland, humbly directing his eyes heavenward and affirming: קטנתי מכל החסדים ומכל האמת אשר עשית את עבדך, "I am unworthy of all the kindness and all the truth that You have shown Your servant" (Genesis 32:11). We tend more often to see the fulfillment of Moses' concern expressed in Deuteronomy 8:12–14: פן תאכל ושבעת ובתים טובים תבנה וישבת וגו׳, "Lest you eat and be satisfied, and you build good houses and settle, and your cattle, sheep, and goats increase, and you increase silver and gold for yourselves, and everything that you have will increase," ורם לבבך ושכחת את א-להיך המוציאך מארץ מצרים מבית עבדים, "...then your heart will become proud and you will forget the Lord your God Who took you out of the land of Egypt, from the house of bondage."

The higher one climbs up the ladder of success and the more gratitude one ought to feel, the easier it is to overlook the guiding hand of God. To oneself one must admit: "I am really no better than my neighbor with whom I grew up and with whom I worked and struggled. I am no more ambitious and capable than he, yet I reached the height of success while he is still at the bottom."

Rarely do we take note of how often success in our secular lives results in a diminution of religious life. We encounter individuals who once walked the path leading to God, and who followed scrupulously the statutes that our religion imposes on us. Yet when fortune shines on them and their debt to the Almighty has increased accordingly, they will attribute success to themselves, their situation in life, and their work, while becoming progressively estranged from God, from their coreligionists, and from the house of worship.

איש כמתנת ידו כברכת וגו׳. Therefore, the message of our religion is "Everyone according to his ability to give, according to the blessing that the Lord, your God, has given you." The higher your achievements in success or wealth, the greater your obligation to thank and venerate God and strengthen your belief in Him. Only with active participation in Jewish religious life can we preserve our Judaism. We must champion our faith and glorify it, whether we are young or old, high or humble. The more lofty our position, the greater is our obligation.

My dear listeners: It is with sad remembrance that we now dedicate our thoughts to the souls of those who have departed. Many will recall in devout prayer their pious fathers and their God-fearing mothers. Their memory will be a special blessing for us if it stimulates us to godly deeds. איש כמתנת ידו –

each according to what he really is and what he does. Let everyone remember, with reverence, his devout parents by seeking to emulate them in their behavior, "each according to his means, according to the blessing that God has bestowed on him." May the parting message of our festival leave a lasting impression on us, and may the remembrance of those who have gone to their eternal home stir us to join the previous generations in our worship of God according to our means, as the Lord has blessed us. Amen.

Youth and Old Age

First Day Pesach 5659 [1899]

If we are to understand the true meaning of Pesach, the Festival of Freedom, which begins today, and view it as an uplifting and ennobling experience for our hearts and spirits, we must ponder over the causes that led to its establishment and look back in time to see what preceded it – the time of our forefathers' enslavement in the land of Egypt.

We are presented with two manifestations. On the one hand we see Pharaoh, the king of Egypt, a cruel and sinister ruler, who, despite his immense and unlimited might, fears the six hundred thousand men who have taken residence in a remote part of his kingdom. He seeks to incite in his people a hatred for the Israelites, pointing to the dangers that these strangers pose to him and to his nation. With self-adulation and a total lack of human feeling, he spins such a fine net of suppression and persecution around these unfortunate people that they become involuntary tools to his outrageous moods.

On the other hand we see the Israelites as dejected and without vigor, offering no resistance to their common enemy, and yet fostering dissension within their own ranks. They show but muffled despair in their deplorable situation, making no effort to improve their lot, yet contending with the very one (Moses) who shows empathy with their affliction (Exodus 2:14). But it was not just the external shackles that kept the people down and impeded their prospering. Much stronger and more unfortunate were the internal, invisible shackles that obstructed the development of their spiritual lives and robbed them of their basic human dignity.

And yet the memory of a majestic line of ancestors was alive among the Israelites. A ray of light from the past would sometimes penetrate the somber present, an occasional star of hope illuminating the sky. Such rays of hope were rare and were usually followed by yet denser darkness.

Finally, as the hour of redemption draws near, the shackles of serfdom are broken, and the oppression comes to an end. The people are now yearning for freedom. And yet, the breaking of these external, visible shackles – with all of Pharaoh's inflexibility and callousness and considering Israel's state of indolence and despondency – was easier than training the people to attain the liberation of their inner life. That would have to await the future for which the פסח לדורות, the Pesach for all time, would be established.

It is therefore of great significance that we observe this annual festival in the same spirit that our forefathers celebrated it in Egypt. For us, too, Pesach must be a celebration of freedom – a festival that provides us with inner spiritual elevation and loosens the chains of evil that surround us.

The Torah has faithfully preserved for us all of the precepts and requirements related to that first Pesach in Egypt. But fundamental to this festival, as it was intended by God, are the words spoken by Moses when he was asked by Pharaoh just who will celebrate this festival: מי ומי ההלכים? (Exodus 10:8) בנערינו ובזקנינו נלך בבנינו ובבנותינו בצאננו ובבקרנו נלך כי חג ה' לנו – "With our young and with our old shall we go, with our sons and with our daughters, with our flock and our cattle shall we go, because it is a festival of the Lord for us" (Exodus 10:9). It is this essential aspect of our festival that we would like today to examine more closely.

My dear listeners, there is hardly a more gratifying observation for our tender emotions than the harmonious interaction of old and young, the two frontiers of human life. The very fact that young and old, differing so much in their outlook and their aspirations, agree to unite for a common cause is all the more pleasing and refreshing.

Youth is the time of joyous hope, high expectations and plans for the distant future. It is a time of storm and stress, an almost unbridled zest for action and creative urge. The youthful spirit seeks to permeate the universe, testing its strengths against the time-proven foundation pillars. Old age, on the other hand, is a time of quiet steadfastness, with little inclination to engage the new and the unknown. The former vigor is lacking, and as we move in our accustomed track, our aspiration is diminished. But old age is also a time of serene judgment. Circumspection replaces youthful impetuosity, clarity of thought and consideration substitutes for vague goals and fanciful ideals.

Total spiritual harmony of the two would hardly be expected or even desired. Nothing repels us more than a senile youth whose excesses consume his warmhearted feelings, nor will the old man who has yet to subdue his youthful impetuousness arouse much favor in us. But when a loving union between the young and the old exists – when they are united in a common cause, with mutual understanding and consideration – they will strive for a common goal. While this is true in many fields, it applies in special measure to our Jewish way of life. Here old and young can stand together in harmony, the old contributing with their mature deliberation, the young with their noble zeal, both reaching towards the same ideal and lofty purpose.

Pharaoh knew full well that he would concede Israel nothing by granting them the permission of לכו נא הגברים ועבדו את ה', "Let the men go and serve the Lord" (Exodus 10:11), by having the elderly go without the youth to celebrate the festival. That kind of service would have been short-lived and would soon dwindle, condemning the people once more to a yoke of slavery. But Moses understood what matters in the religious life of the people. He countered Pharaoh's proposal with the words: בנערינו ובזקנינו נלך, "With our young and with our old shall we go" – both were to draw near to God, both reaching for the lofty goal of conducting their lives in a way pleasing to Him and worshiping Him with piety. Only in this way would Israel be able to shed their yoke of slavery and face their destiny.

There is a profound truth in the story of our sages that the Lord would hand over His Torah on Mount Sinai only when Israel was prepared to present their children as guarantors for their observance of His commandments (*Song of Songs Rabbah* 1:4). Indeed, only when parents make their children the guarantors for the preservation of God's commandments, teaching them to maintain and cherish their faith, can we feel assured about the security of Israel and its Torah. Every generation presents a new group of protectors of the faith, every time period has its multitudes of guardians of our religion. And the promise that Israel made to God at Mount Sinai is seeing its fulfillment in our very day. The father sees his faithful son espousing the religion of his forefathers. With joyful readiness the child grasps the thread of faith slipping away from the tired hands of his dying forefathers, only to continue spinning it according to the examples and impressions gained from previous generations.

Consider the progenitor of our lineage, Abraham. His was the onerous mandate to offer up to the Lord his one and only son, for whom he had hoped for so long and whom he loved fervently. Approaching the place where he and his lad were bidden to go, he ascended the mountain to the site that had been selected for the sacrifice, his boy walking by his side in equal devotion and piety. וילכו שניהם יחדו, "And the two of them went together" (Genesis 22:6, 8) – Scripture repeats it twice, father and son both guided by the same desire to carry out God's will.

Proceeding further into the history of our people, we meet a venerable priest, Judah the Maccabee, in a small town near Jerusalem. He had refused to obey the tyrannical command of the pagan king to prostrate himself before an idol that had been erected. Together with his five like-minded sons, he exacted bloody vengeance on the enemy hordes that had sought his demise and that of his home. Though very old, he drew his sword in defense of his country's freedom and the preservation of his religion. He was unable to carry out his work of liberation to its conclusion, death having called a halt to his striving – but a glance at his sons enabled him to depart peacefully from this world, secure in the knowledge that as long as such men champion Israel, Judaism will never become extinct.

Such phenomena in the course of Israel's history were seen in every generation and in every land. The battle cry was always בנערינו ובזקנינו נלך – "With our young and with our old shall we go!" Fathers would not countenance their children cutting themselves off from their people via apostasy in order to lighten their life's burden and spare them discrimination and persecution. No! Better that they and their family suffer the most severe affliction, even to perish, rather than cause an unbridgeable chasm between themselves and their parents, between themselves and their coreligionists. So have Jews acted throughout the ages.

It is fortunate that today, as well, such contrary behavior is but rarely seen except among those whom we can no longer count as ours. What we do find more frequently within our ranks is a lamentable indifference to what we should regard as sacred and lofty, an indifference to the fostering and preservation of religion in the hearts of our children. It is such indifference that can lead to the deplorable situation that we have described: apostasy.

Parents therefore cannot be content merely to show themselves receptive to their religion. To a much greater extent, parents must bear in mind the guarantees that Israel bore at Sinai, and guide their children to value their religion and to participate actively in religious life. Only then will they prove themselves serious minded in their avowal, and bequeath unto their children that religious feeling they received from their fathers. Only then will they have discharged their religious duty.

חנך לנער על פי דרכו גם כי יזקין לא יסור ממנה – "Train the youth in the way he should go; even when he gets old he will not depart from it" (Proverbs 22:6). Such is the advice of the wise King Solomon. This must be accomplished with pious and convincing zeal, otherwise the little sprig of religious belief will not grow deep roots into the heart of the growing child, and might yet wilt completely. Such a total lack of appreciation of what was holy for our fathers can lead to the disastrous view expressed by the prophet Malachi (3:14): שוא עבד א-להים ומה בצע כי שמרנו משמרתו, "It is useless to serve God; what gain is there for us that we have kept His precepts?"

Such a state of affairs cannot but have its effect on the immediate family. In former days the devotion that the sons and daughters of Israel held for their parents was legendary and exemplary, manifesting not only in life but even extending beyond the grave decades after the parents had departed to the beyond. Nowadays such attitudes are rapidly dwindling, as any perceptive observer will note. Parental respect, formerly among the noblest of flowers in the wreath of our virtues, has all too often been replaced by insolence and arrogance, thereby weakening the pillars that support family life. That sacred spiritual harmony, the invisible bond joining the hearts of parents and children in common aspirations and goals – these are missing.

My devout listeners: The Midrash describes that when Israel in the wilderness wanted to erect the sanctuary and all had been prepared, the individual pieces did not fit and could not be joined, threatening that ornate edifice with ruin before it was ever completed. Then came Moses and arranged all the parts in such a way that they were able to join together by themselves. Nowadays, in the small sanctuaries that are our family dwellings, and which are intended as models of the Divine habitation in the midst of the camp of Israel, the individual components no longer fit together as well as when the structure of the Jewish family was more secure. It is here that the teachings of Moses can help in uniting the hearts and minds of the children with the hearts and minds of their fathers, so that the original sanctity and warmth can once again pervade the tents of Jacob.

May this festival of Pesach, which we celebrate בנערינו ובזקנינו, "with our young and with our old," pave the way to improving ourselves. May its manifold symbolism motivate parents to imbue the hearts of their children with love for God and for our faith, so that this holiday will indeed be a festival of freedom and redemption. May God so grant. Amen.

The Family Celebration

First Day Pesach 5662 [1902]

כי הנה הסתו עבר הגשם חלף הלך לו
"For, lo, the winter is past, the rain is over and gone."
הנצנים נראו בארץ עת הזמיר הגיע
"The flowers appear on the earth, the time of singing has come"
(Song of Songs 2:11–12).

Our own feelings are mirrored in this joyful, springtime declaration from Song of Songs, as we observe Nature blossoming forth its buds, and we see fields and meadows covered, as if by a magical hand, in a festive floral garb. As the soft breezes of spring blow once again, and the iron shackles of winter that had held Nature tightly enclosed have loosened, we feel – in our hearts – a deep sense of renewed growth. The melodious sounds of springtime resonate with a thousand echoes in the chords of our hearts, and the clear blue of a cloudless sky finds a friendly reflection in our souls.

And with this mood of hope, joy, and spiritual elevation comes a shout of jubilation from an ancient source: הנה הסתו עבר, "For lo, the winter is past... the time of singing has come." It is a cry from the vaulted halls of our past and from the winding corridors of our history, a sound issuing forth from the memory of an event incomparable in its form, its result, and its consequences. There, in the distant fields of our forefathers' history, we detect a process of budding, flowering, and growth, the gentle touch of spring blowing upon us. It is the spring of a nation in its very beginnings. And a magnificent springtime it was indeed, no less saturated with sunshine and flowers than the awakening of Nature, as Israel was shaken from its centuries-long winter slumber of Pharaoh's enslavement.

At this time of our Pesach festival, we hear the resounding of two voices of spring: the spring of Nature and the spring of our people coming to life. We sense the former in what we observe and contemplate; the latter resides in our collective memory. Again and again, the recollection of the Exodus is the salient point of departure in the Torah's teaching and admonishments. It is a recurrent theme in our prayers and forms a daily part of our spiritual being. The totality of the Exodus's value has yet to be fully described, and its source of delight, even today, is not exhausted.

Today we want to direct our attention to but one of the manifold aspects of the Exodus from Egypt: namely, Moses' initial call concerning the very first celebration of Pesach in Egypt, which was to serve as the ideal model of how we are to make this festival meaningful for all time: ויקרא משה לכל זקני ישראל ויאמר אלהם משכו וקחו לכם צאן למשפחתיכם ושחטו הפסח, "Moses called to all of the elders of Israel and said to them, 'Draw forth and take for yourselves sheep for your families and slaughter the Pesach offering'" (Exodus 12:21). It is this verse that will be the subject of our consideration.

You might well think, my listeners, that this precept has no present-day value or relevance for us. No longer do we prepare a Paschal lamb, nor do we have an altar upon which to offer it. The literal fulfillment of this Divine precept, as enunciated by Moses, had already become an impossibility when the Temple in Jerusalem was destroyed. With sadness, Israel carried with it the memory of the former Temple service in its wanderings across the face of the earth. And yet, there is one word that retains its full meaning for us today, one word that has retained the full impact of its admonition and significance. Let us take it to heart as one of the prime goals of our Pesach festival. Although our way of observing Pesach has changed over the centuries, it is the reference to למשפחתיכם – to celebrate this festival within your family circle, to celebrate it for your family – that retains its undiminished strength, whether applied to the tormented Jewish slaves in Pharaoh's land or to the free children of Israel in our own time.

It is telling for our entire Jewish outlook on life that the first precept that Israel, collectively, received from God would find its fulfillment within the confines of the family. This precept was directed in its full measure toward the future preservation of the purity and the sanctity of the family. It was according to their families that Israel encamped in the desert. The numbers of men eligible for military duty were recorded according to the families, and the Levites were conscripted for service in the sanctuary according to their families. No, the warmth of Jewish family life, which is nothing short of proverbial, is not fortuitous. It emanates from the regulations laid down by our religion and the lofty instructions found in God's teachings.

And yet, why talk of the instructions and direction of the laws when life itself speaks so clearly and eloquently, and when history depicts, in an ideal manner, the personification of all that the law aims to achieve? The family is the foundation of national life. From the fertile ground of the family sprouts every noble virtue, producing industry and moderation, as well as self-sacrifice and self-denial. It breeds love for the surrounding community and loyalty to the fatherland. As long as the sanctity of the family is maintained, a people's existence is secure, despite attempts at suppression by outside enemies and destruction of political independence.

And in all this, Israel is a living and eloquent example. It was not a caprice of fate that Israel, its state in ruins and its homeland lost, has survived to this very day – not weakened or broken, but rather full of moral vigor and cheerful optimism. Israel surmounted victoriously the most severe suffering and the bloodiest persecution, even if with tearful eyes and heavy hearts. Throughout the millennia, as our people were suppressed and hounded by their neighbors, the family was the paradise in which the Jew took refuge. At its gates, the angel of God, fiery sword in hand, stood guard, repelling the hostile forms of hate and slander, and replacing in bountiful manner the fruits that the outside world denied them. While outside hatred was threatening and the enemy lay in ambush, the reviled Jew, within the confines of his home, experienced human dignity, happy in seeing his image reflected in the loving eyes of his family and recognizing in their glances true mutual love.

What, then, was the driving element – that binding glue – within Jewish family life? By what means did our people succeed in maintaining their strength and exerting their moral influence on all family members? That foundation was laid in Egypt, and it extended magnificently throughout the later life of the Jewish people. למשפחתיכם, "Take for yourselves a lamb for your family," was God's instruction that Moses transmitted to Israel, so that in later years, the father of the house could portray to his attentive children בעבור זה עשה ה' לי בצאתי ממצרים, "It is because of this that the Lord acted on my behalf when I left Egypt" (Exodus 13:8); ולכל בני ישראל היה אור במושבתם, "For all of the Children of Israel there was light in their dwellings" (Exodus 10:23). It was a light not just kindled during the darkness of Egyptian slavery, but throughout the ages, when men's lives became so darkened by lack of mutual kindness that they could no longer see each other.

In Israel's dwellings, the family table became the altar, their home a substitute for the destroyed sanctuary. Their hearts became holy arks, the voices of their children evoked the chorus of Levites singing the highest praises to God, and the bread became the shewbread for the eternal God. This consecration of the home engendered the encouragement and strength necessary to surmount all danger and survive all persecution. The harsh hand of the enemy could snatch away national independence and political freedom, but no cunning or evil could to rob the Jew of his family life, a life grounded in the belief in God. In localities where Jews enjoyed but brief repose, where their property and belongings were plundered and they were expelled, naked, from their places of sojourn, the intimacy of the family remained intact, because it was based on belief in God. Were one to say that Israel's only striving was for material goods, the holy atmosphere of home and family would give the lie to this accusation. In the Jewish home resides an ideal world where life is imbued with spiritual content, where existence on this earth has a higher purpose.

What comparisons with the present time can we make? Perhaps you might do well to ask this of yourselves. Consider whether your family life is suffused with godliness and directed to a higher aim and purpose. Is it structured on the basis of the unshakeable foundation of our holy teachings? Only if our family life remains pure, pious, and holy can we face the future with comfort and serenity. As long as the family serves as the repository of our religion, we need not fear for Judaism's continuity.

מה טבו אהליך יעקב משכנתיך ישראל, "How beautiful are your tents, O Jacob, your dwellings, O Israel" (Numbers 24:5), declared Balaam, the heathen impulses of her heart, she kindled in her children's souls the love of God, even when death was imminent. Calmly she urged them to submit to the sword of the oppressor, fearing only that this horrible agony might possibly shake their faith in the Almighty.

With the same love for their faith, millions of mothers in Israel have proven themselves in times of persecution, when the choice was between apostasy and death. They chose death because death was life for them, whereas life without their faith was death. O, let us peruse these blood-stained annals, not to fill our hearts with pain or with hate for the torturers, but rather to see in these pages of history a model of unshakable faith and steadfastness in trying times – so that you, of this generation, might fan the smoldering sparks of religious inspiration into a bright flame. That flame will warm our hearts and inspire steadfast faith in our God and our religion.

Much have the women of Israel done to maintain our religion and our people. And had their deeds been limited only to the tranquility of family life, their actions would nevertheless have had their effect in the public sphere, stimulating, encouraging, calming, and blessing. Where did the hounded and persecuted Jew of the Middle Ages find those rays of sun that allowed him to forget his suffering and experience solace from discrimination and persecution? From where did he muster the strength to renew his almost hopeless struggle with a superior enemy, and where did he find empathy and understanding for his struggles and his goals? Was it not there where he found a congenial and sympathetic soul, a loving wife who afforded him the strength and courage to persist and gave him a feeling of human dignity? Denied the pleasures of the outside world, he finds noble bliss in the sanctity of his family life. The more he is despised and reviled outside, the more intense his domestic joy.

And now, dear women and mothers of Israel, can you view yourselves as reflections of these noble women of yesteryear? If you can claim to have accepted the legacy of your female ancestors, albeit in different times and circumstances but with the same love and devotion, then you will be doing what the mothers of Israel did in the land of Egypt: to guarantee the preservation and continuity of our people Israel. For Judaism, even in our modern times, still draws its strength and vigor from the same bedrock of family life. Now, as do you rather find yourselves estranged from the women of old? The calling of Israel's women today is what it has been throughout the centuries, and the continuity of our people is assured so long as Jewish women understand their historic role.

My dear listeners, it was more than just a momentary inspiration that made our sages declare: בזכות נשים צדקניות נגאלו אבותינו ממצרים, "In the merit of the righteous women was Israel redeemed from Egypt" (Talmud Bavli, *Sotah* 11b). This declaration was based on the consideration of the lives of the Jews in Egypt in that period of time and even earlier. Our sages recognized the major contribution that women made toward the preservation of Israel, the maintenance of Israel's special purity and singular character within a hostile environment, their worship of the one God, and the devout attachment of children to their parents. It was the women, no less than the men, who determined the future character of Israel. Along with our three patriarchs, who laid the groundwork of our belief in the one God, stood our four mothers, who lovingly nurtured this belief. Side by side with Moses and Aaron, who, to the fullest extent of their personalities, interceded on behalf of Israel, stands Moses' mother, brave and energetic, countering the savage command of Pharaoh in order to save her infant son; and Miriam, the prophetess, who with loving eye stood watch over her brother at the river's bank, and who later grasped the drum at the time of Israel's deliverance at the Red Sea to inspire the Israelite women to praise the Lord in song.

In later times, when the princes of Israel slackened in their leadership and surrendered to the assaults of their arrogant enemies, it was a woman, the prophetess Deborah, "mother in Israel," who came to the rescue. Grasping sword and spear, and with her fiery spirit and courage, she animated the men to engage the enemy. The later history of the Jews is filled with similar acts. A Syrian king brought Judah to its knees: with arrogant self-adulation, he sought to replace God's commandments with his own, so that Israel would renounce everything that was sacred to them and their forefathers. It was a frail woman, Hannah, mother of seven sturdy sons, who would teach the king that though he might massacre Israel, never would he sever them from their faith in God. Subduing her motherly love and desperately fighting the

The Merit of the Pious Women

Second Day Pesach 5659 [1899]

The piety of our sages and their great reverence for our traditions manifests itself to a large extent in their efforts to explore, in the minutest detail, those momentous events of the past that had special significance in the development of the Jewish people. At the same time, they strove to uncover particularly those details that brought about these events, and to ascribe significance to their occurrence. This special love and devotion is well seen in their description of the Exodus from Egypt. With remarkable fervor, our sages immersed themselves in the analysis of the subtlest hints found in Scripture, often taking a single word as a point of reference for thoughtful consideration, and painting luminous pictures that allow us to view the details of our liberation from Egyptian slavery. What Scripture did not tell us was often related by means of Aggadic embellishment.

Our sages pondered over what made Israel worthy of Divine redemption, and with remarkable expertise they saw in Israel's life in Egypt the seeds and beginnings of those virtues that would, in later times, manifest themselves with such splendor. The fact that the Israelites distinguished themselves from the surrounding heathen world was what lent them their uncompromising steadfastness and indestructible stability. Our sages felt that it was this distinctness from the Egyptians that made Israel worthy of Divine help.

Let us, today, scrutinize specifically the qualities attributed to the Jewish women during their sojourn in Egypt, qualities that protected our people from destruction and brought on their deliverance. In doing so, we also wish to pose to our women of today the question: Have you remained faithful to the examples of your ancestors, and do you see yourselves in their image? Or seer, upon observing Israel's family life in its intimacy, holiness, and dedication to the service of God. So can our houses be deserving of such description if we regard ourselves as encamping round the Tabernacle, as did our forefathers in the desert, and allow God to lead us through life's paths; if we consider our table an altar, and the hearts of our family members as holy arks containing the teachings of the God of Israel.

My devout listeners: It is, above all, למשפחתיכם – within the family circle – that Israel celebrates its festival of Pesach. May all our festivals imbue our family life with such holiness as will link the hearts of fathers with those of their forefathers, and the hearts of children with those of their fathers in the upholding of our sacred faith. Today, as throughout the millennia, it will strengthen us, elevate us beyond the worldly, and unite us with the eternal God. Amen.

in former days, Judaism can flourish and blossom only when firmly grounded in family life guided by the woman of the home.

And though a man needs to struggle in the outside world for his existence, and sometimes has to make certain compromises, no matter how justified, the Jewish family life must always remain intact. It is here that women must take on the role of devout priestesses, maintaining the flame of religion on the altar of the home where the holy fire of religion and the fear of God hold sway. Here Jewish women greet the Sabbath with the radiant light of their candles and glorify the festivals, even if the man of the house believes himself compelled not to interrupt his daily struggle for existence. Here the mother should direct her children's gaze heavenward and seek to instill holiness in their hearts. It is here that Jewish women must prove themselves worthy of their good name, and demonstrate, by deed, that the calling of Jewish women is not so much to radiate glory to the exterior, but rather to exert their influence in the home, just as their pious mothers did in Egypt.

My dear listeners, when God was about to reveal himself to Israel on Mount Sinai, Moses was instructed to transmit His message first to the women and then to the men (Rashi, Exodus 19:3). "Why first to the women?" ask our sages, and they answer: כדי שיהו מנהיגות את בניהם לתורה, "Since it was their primary obligation to direct their children's hearts to the service of God's Torah" (Rabbeinu Bachya, Exodus 19:3).

May you women and mothers fully appreciate this most delightful and beautiful duty, and always practice it with holy zeal. Then can Israel face the future confidently, and it will be said about you: "In the merit of the pious women will Israel be preserved." Amen.

The Jewish Heart

Seventh Day Pesach 5662 [1902]

My devout listeners: today we shall reflect on the words of that magnificent book of our Holy Scriptures entitled "Song of Songs." Originally, this book was approached with misgiving and contempt, and was not considered worthy of being included in the canon of sacred scriptures. However, when our sages immersed themselves in the study of this work, recognized its lofty poetic value, and gained insight into its incomparable beauty, the book attained such significance as to be called, of all the holy books of the Bible, the holiest. Religious custom determined, early on, that it be read on Pesach, the Festival of Spring, since Song of Songs is permeated by the sweetest scent of spring, and animated by its sunny breath. We observe nature's awakening, see the blossoming of fragrant flowers, and hear the lively song of little birds. Fields and meadows unfold before us as we walk through green vineyards and shady orchards. Rolling, seeded fields and meadows decorated with flowers stretch out before our feet in the radiance of spring's magic. But what really lends this charming picture its incomparable appeal is the animated, ecstatic song of humankind.

A young man seeks his dearly beloved, hurrying after her through smiling fields, and depicting her as gracious, charming, and delightful as only true love can see it. And she, whom he eagerly seeks, flirts with him in an amorous play that betrays a heartfelt yearning.

A unique charm pervades this attractive book which we designate, in our German language, with the special term *"das hohe Lied"* (high song), whereas in the Hebrew language it is more appropriately called שיר השירים, Song of Songs.

Our sages described this Song as קודש קדשים, possessing a most extraordinary sanctity. In their deeply religious spirit, they regarded the gracious maiden, whose praise her lover sang with such magnificent tones, as symbolizing the community of Israel. In her loving friend they recognized the benevolent God, who had chosen Israel as His bride, and who rendered to her affection as only a bridegroom is capable of doing. This apt metaphor by our sages was not at all artificial or far-fetched, being rather grounded in their mental attitude, but also substantiated by the Song itself.

It is not our purpose today to delineate in detail just how we recognize in the Shulammite, that delightful maiden, characteristics that define the essence of our people. We will rather direct our attention to a pronouncement made by the Shulammite that offers us a clear insight into her spiritual life and reveals her hidden sentiments. אני ישנה ולבי ער, "I sleep, but my heart is awake" (Song of Songs 5:2). Thus declares the Shulammite, revealing that her love for the one she has chosen never slumbers, though her exterior may seem cold and without feeling. Our sages have applied this phrase – אני ישנה ולבי ער , "I sleep but my heart is awake" – to Israel, and it speaks to our present generation as well. Let us try to qualify it and investigate its significance and value.

My devout listeners: We hear much these days about the Jewish heart, a term that has become almost proverbial. We extol it as a priceless possession, an inalienable inheritance of our people. When concerned with deeds of kindness, to act nobly and with goodness, to bring about blessing, to dry painful tears, and to alleviate undeserved suffering – there the warm, feeling, sympathetic Jewish heart manifests itself as incapable of remaining indifferent to human misery. That is the Jewish heart, the tradition of our people not to remain idle when action is needed. Yet we must understand this chiefly in the sense that it was acquired, from time immemorial, from the example of our ancestors and the teachings of our Torah. Behold Abraham, "the rock out of which we were hewn, the source from which we were created" (Isaiah 51:1). His conduct was unique in his time, and all of his noble deeds which we admire today had their source in his warm, sympathetic heart. It is these qualities of Abraham that the Torah especially sought to awaken in his descendents. Abraham taught us that God's providence extends not only to our neighboring countrymen but to all humanity, even the animals and inanimate plants.

Our sages regarded the "Jewish heart" as applying to all phases of life, the source of all things good and noble, the beautiful and the sublime. From the Jewish heart emanates reverence for God, kindness to fellow creatures, obedience and fidelity, devotion and piety. The tender words of Midrash Shir Hashirim (5:2) read: אמרה כנסת ישראל לפני הקב״ה: רבונו של עולם אני ישנה מן המצות ולבי ער לגמלות חסדים, אני ישנה מן הקרבנות ולבי ער לקריאת שמע ולתפלה – "Said the community of Israel before the Holy One, blessed be He: 'Sovereign of the Universe! Though I am asleep in the performance of my religious obligations, my heart is awake for the performance of charity. Though I am asleep in respect to the sacrifices, my heart is awake for the recital of Shema and prayer.'"

Indeed, even when the Jewish heart is not occupied in the fulfillment of mitzvot, one can still recognize it in its performance of good deeds. When the Jewish community, after the destruction of the Temple, could no longer bring sacrifices, the Jewish heart found a substitute in the form of prayer and the study of God's teachings. As suffering inflicted upon Israel became more and more pressing, the Jewish heart clung with yet greater enthusiasm to its God, gaining renewed courage and hope. The Jewish heart never slept! And where it slacked off in one endeavor, it embraced another with still greater devotion. Its love and devotion to the Almighty were never in question.

In our day we also take pride in our Jewish hearts. And if one sometimes observes this as the mouthing of empty words, we can point to the tried and proven Jewish heart of the millennia, which was not content with just words but rather with deeds.

In the meantime, my listeners, do we not notice in some circles that the "Jewish heart" has become a mere catchword, its significance so overrated that it has lost its true inner significance? The reference to one's Jewish heart is being sought as a substitute for so many things. Has it become the only sign of attachment to our Jewish community, so that one would declare, "I am a Jew at heart, though I don't manifest it outwardly. It therefore matters not how I stand in relation to my faith and my coreligionists"? Can we not compare this to the miser who boasts of a charitable heart but keeps his hand tightly shut, or the wicked person who claims to have a pure and virtuous heart? Inner feelings count only when they lead to joyful deeds.

What does our Midrash say? "Though I am asleep concerning religious observance, my heart is awake for the performance of charity. Though I am asleep in respect to the sacrifices, my heart is awake for the recital of Shema and prayer." In one way or another the Jewish heart must manifest itself. If it is sleeping in the fulfillment of mitzvot, it must at least practice good deeds. If it is sleeping as concerns visits to the house of God, it should at least maintain its warm feeling for our holy scriptures. Judaism depends on the active participation of its members. When that is not the case, no pretty words or inner feelings will avail. It is only deeds that beget deeds. Mere sentiments do not stimulate emulation, and they are anyway soon extinguished. Therefore if you are to sing the praises of your Jewish heart, let your conduct prove it, and your deeds bear testimony. Our times demand that we vigorously champion our cause.

אני ישנה ולבי ער, "I sleep but my heart is awake." Let this pronouncement of the Shulammite serve as Israel's motto. May we recognize that those outside of our congregation who feel themselves slipping away from our religion may yet retain enough inner vitality and vigor to be inspired by a sublime belief in God and His holy writings, and an appreciation for the incomparable Jewish past. Let these never be empty words. Let our actions and our behavior proclaim conspicuously and undeniably that in our inner being resides a genuine, warm Jewish heart. Amen.

Israel's Victory and Song

Eighth Day Pesach 5659 [1899]

The closing festival of our Pesach holiday presents us with the last act of a tremendous drama, which began in Egypt and ended with the Israelites standing before the Red Sea. During these last days of our festival, our thoughts transport us to the site of our unforgettable liberation from Egypt. We are led into the camp of the endangered Israelites, as well as into the midst of the pursuing Egyptians. Together with the account in yesterday's Torah reading, so lovingly and carefully depicted, we appear today not just as observers but as actual participants in these events.

Our ancestry, as well as our feelings and emotions, place us squarely on the side of the pursued. Eight days ago we imagined embarking on our journey, as we left the country of our serfdom, eating unleavened bread and symbolic bitter herbs. Now, as Israel is once again distressed and threatened with a disastrous fate even greater than the previous one – we share in their trepidation. And as we see salvation finally accomplished, our voices join with their millions in a song of jubilation, a song that not only reverberated into the desert and across the torrents of raging seas, but whose sound has been heard throughout the flight of time, and is recited daily in Israel's houses of worship.

That song, which permeated the entire world, should evoke in us, as well, that same feeling from which it initially emanated, the very feeling that our ancestors experienced at the Red Sea. Though this song initially served as the glorification of God when Israel walked through the Red Sea, as well as an expression of punishment for the Egyptians, its basic mood and thought articulate the sentiments that reverberate through every religious heart. And he who could not join with Israel at the Red Sea singing the words עזי וזמרת י-ה, ויהי לי לישועה, "The Eternal is my might and song, and He has become my salvation" (Exodus 15:2) – his belief in God had not as yet taken firm roots, and his religion had not yet become an intimate part of him. Let us then choose this theme for further contemplation, so that we might recognize how belief in God can become an intimate part of our lives.

My devout listeners, upon reading these words, one might well think: Surely, Israel was able to sing at the Red Sea, since God had championed their cause in an incomparably miraculous manner never recorded in the history of any other nation. Therefore was Israel able to intone this song of victory in praise of God's salvation, and we ourselves would, no doubt, have reacted in the same way. But what of the present time? Ours is not an age of miracles; the sea does not split for us, nor are we guided by pillars of clouds and fire.

And yet, it is only a superficial view of our people's history that would lead one to ask this question. Did we not today, and throughout the eight days of Pesach, join with the psalmist in reciting Hallel and proclaiming those auriferous words: אודך כי עניתני ותהי לי לישועה, "I thank You for You have answered me and have become my salvation" (Psalms 118:21). Likewise, in today's Haftarah, the prophet Isaiah anticipates Israel's words: אודך ה' כי אנפת בי, "I thank You, O God, although You were angry with me," followed by these words of praise to God: הנה א-ל ישועתי אבטח ולא אפחד כי עזי וזמרת י-ה ה' ויהי לי לישועה, "Behold, God is my salvation, I shall trust and not fear; for God the Lord is my might and my song, He has become my salvation" (Isaiah 12:1, 2). No, not just in time of victory did Israel sing praises to God. For had it been only the physical well-being of Israel and its devotion to God and their religion that animated this song at the Red Sea, it would have remained separate and unique, and not found its thousand-fold echo in the songs of the psalmists, in the words of the prophets, and in the pages of our history. For rarely did Israel collectively achieve such spiritual heights. Even when Israel dwelled within the borders of their God-given land, it was not often that everyone lived in peace, each under his vine and his fig tree.

We have here the very secret of our existence and the preservation of our belief. Our devotion to God has remained firm, whether a loving sun smiled upon us from blue skies, or we lived in the shadow of the valley of death. God has ever been our rod and support, and our devotion to Him was all the more firm during times of distress, suffering, and oppression. Not because God was our salvation was He our victory and song, but rather because this song was dedicated to Him for eternity did He become our salvation.

Look back at antiquity when Israel's first national catastrophe struck. The Temple went up in flames, the capital was destroyed, and the people were exiled, by decree of the enemy, to Babylon. At that very time of banishment, when they felt God forsaken and utterly hapless, as Psalm 137 recounts, Israel fervently devoted themselves to God, as they always had done.

Even in misery and defeat was God Israel's victory and song, and that became their salvation, paving the way for their second deliverance, the rebuilding of the Temple, and becoming a people once again. Events at later times proved to be similar, as Jews were scattered across the entire earth, hounded from land to land, expelled from one nation to another. Is our preservation as a people any less miraculous than what occurred at the Red Sea? Perhaps the greatest wonder that ever took place is the continuous existence of our people under circumstances unfavorable beyond imagination.

And should you ask what guarded Israel from the ruin that befell even the mightiest nations, there is but one answer: "God is my victory and song, and He has become my salvation." This was the bond that united the scattered ranks of our people, the magic spell that steeled the nerves and lent hope and courage to our lives.

Yea, that song was sung amidst the deepest pain, and no amount of suffering could still it. Though hearts were broken and life threatened to slip away, that song was not interrupted. It resounded in the houses of God, in family homes, at the cradle and at the grave, sung by men, women, lads and lasses, children and the aged. Not only with their mouths but also with their hearts did they sing this song, as well as through their deeds and the conduct of their lives, their sentiments, and their aspirations.

Behold Rabbi Akivah, that wise, sharp-witted teacher, imprisoned by the Romans and condemned to burn at the stake because he sought to spread the teachings of the Torah. While the flames were already licking at him, and the angels on high were bringing their complaint before the throne of the Supreme Judge – זו תורה וזו שכרה, "Is this the Torah, and is this its reward?" (Talmud

Bavli, *Berachot* 61b) – Rabbi Akivah never wavered in his belief; his trust in God was unshakable. God was his victory even when he had to submit to his enemies and the flames engulfed him, and he intoned that jubilant call שמע ישראל ה׳ א-להינו ה׳ אחד, "Hear, O Israel, the Lord your God, the Lord is One."

Three hundred thousand Jews left the sunny fields of Spain in 1492 because they would not forsake their God. They were forbidden to take along any of their possessions, save for the memories of those golden years they and their forefathers had enjoyed there. The future they faced held nothing in store but deprivation and misery, yet at no time was the loyalty to their belief in question. The Talmud Bavli in *Pesachim* 87b describes the two broken tablets at Mount Sinai: לוחות נשברו ואותיות פורחות, "The tablets were broken but the letters soared upwards." So it occurred in this and all other persecutions to which Israel was subjected: individual persons perished, but the spirit that animated them and the teachings that they represented were preserved. Israel was victorious even in its downfall.

And herein, my devout listeners, we do not quite measure up to our ancestors. Thank God, our loyalty is not put to the test under the same bitter circumstances that our forefathers experienced. Most fortunate this is indeed, for who knows, were we so subjected, whether we would endure such a trial, and whether our spirits would be as firm as in days gone by. We no longer possess the strength to be tolerant, the courage to deny ourselves, and the ability of self-control. In contrast to our ancestors, our resolute championing of our faith is often shaky. While we also want to sing עזי וזמרת י-ה, "God is my victory and my song," we harbor some mental reservation concerning ויהי לי לישועה, "He has become my salvation." Let me not be limited in my comforts, and let my tranquility not be disturbed. I want no demands made on me in the form of self-conquest or self-denial. The ancient song has lost its original vigor and now seems soft and timid.

How then can this song become a salvation for you, salvation resulting from the victory of the lofty over the base, the godly over what is mortal and transitory? The Yizkor service we are about to intone might allow you to experience this. With deep emotion you remember at this time those dearly beloved who have passed on, and for whom you yearn. Your eyes are filled with tears, your hearts with sadness. It is here that our religion becomes manifest, reminding you with love and comfort that God is your victory and song. Turn your gaze from the past to eternity, from this world of pretense to a higher and more noble existence. You will then be able to surmount your grief and attain renewed hope and confidence. As you direct your praises to God, your suffering will be vanquished; as you humbly subjugate yourself to Him, you will be uplifted. May your efforts be rewarded, and may you be inspired by this festival to choose as the guiding principle governing your life: עזי וזמרת י-ה ויהי לי לישועה.

May this be God's will. Amen.

THE GOD OF THE FATHERS

Eighth Day Pesach 5663 [1903]

Immense and overwhelming as the liberation from Egypt is, as it unfolds before our eyes on the first days of our festival, the phenomenon that the closing days of our festival recalls assumes an even greater dimension. Not that the splitting of the Red Sea was a greater miracle than the breaking of the shackles of Egyptian slavery. For God's limitless omnipotence, there are no gradations of what is possible. Our sages say that the rise skyward and descent to earth of a drop of water in its varying states is as much a miracle as the colossal parting of the waters that today's festival recalls.

And yet there is something special that lends the events at the Red Sea their sublime eminence. It occurred at that moment when Israel's spiritual life first began to shine in its full glory. For this event, Israel required no preliminary instruction from Moses on how to serve God. Out of the depth of their grateful hearts gushed forth an inspired song, like a mighty mountain stream making its way through a crevice. How did it come to pass that Israel had now become so transformed? What evoked such an epochal change? How did Israel, just released from slavery, suddenly become a nation of singers?

The people were swept along by events whose imprint exerted a powerful influence on them. It was at the Red Sea that Israel, on their own, arrived at an understanding of Moses' first message to them – the message that the Almighty, the God of their fathers, would always be at their side. With great rapture, their lips intoned: זה א-לי ואנוהו א-להי אבי וארממנהו, "This is my God and I will glorify Him, the God of my father and I will exalt Him" (Exodus 15:2). Our sages ascribe these words to the children singing in praise of God's splitting of the sea and sending the Egyptians to the bottom of the abyss (Talmud Bavli, *Ketubot* 7b). Can our youth, nowadays, also intone these inspired words, and choose as their guiding principle the words א-להי אבי וארממנהו – "I will praise and exalt the God of my father"? And yet, it is in the application of these words that we can discover the secret of Israel's strength and permanence, as we shall try to demonstrate today.

My devout listeners: The admonitions promulgated to Israel to follow God's commandments and walk in His ways have always had a moving and powerful effect on the Jewish people. And yet, blind faith and unconditional acceptance without full conviction was never demanded of us. The people were not to be held in spiritual semidarkness or entrust themselves to strange ways, but rather to be able to declare זה א-לי, "This is my God and indeed I recognize Him." Thus it is every father's duty to show his child the source of this doctrine, so that he may see it clearly, rather than believe it blindly.

"Knowledge and perception are important," say our sages, "since God Himself is called the God of Knowledge in our Scriptures." Not blind faith but rather knowledge and perception are required of us, as we read in Ethics of the Fathers (2:6), אין בור ירא חטא, "The ignorant cannot be fearful of sin." Therefore the dissemination of religious knowledge has long been regarded by Jews as a sacred obligation that did not require the mandate of a government. It was rather the loving parental care that planted the seeds of religious knowledge, which then grew into a mighty tree of faith that was able to withstand the mightiest of storms.

At one time, we regarded our ability to disseminate the knowledge of Judaism without outside help or governmental support as a great privilege. Sadly, this privilege is being felt today as a disadvantage, in that we are forced to look to the authorities when it concerns implanting religion into the hearts of our children.

To what extent do we devote any serious effort in cultivating the knowledge of religion? To be sure we still bring our young boys to the Torah, having prepared them for their bar-mitzvah celebration. And yet, what once was a time of consecration, a resolve to attaining deeper knowledge, the beginning of thorough searching, has today become, for too many, a sort of "farewell to Torah." With the bar-mitzvah celebration we have rendered proper due to our religion – "Our boy recited the *berachah* over the Torah flawlessly and said the Haftarah without mistakes, which, for our day and age, is enough. After all, he does not aspire to be a Jewish scholar, nor need he be strictly religious, since we, his parents, are not." How strange that Jewish parents constantly strive to see their children surpass them in knowledge, so that they might attain intellectual enrichment in all fields – all fields, that is, except in the realm of religion, where expectations are but modest and are limited to what is deemed most essential.

While religious knowledge rarely brings with it material blessing, it does provide spiritual enrichment and ennoblement of the soul. Besides, dear parents, do Religious-Liberals not require religious knowledge? Do they not, more than others, need to acquire insight into our religious sources to enable them to distinguish the essentials from what is less significant? Or are we to equate Religious Liberalism with thoughtlessness and limited knowledge? Can these individuals see themselves as "enlightened" when they no longer regard this or that statute as important, or speak with disdain and with superficial knowledge about matters they do not understand? Do not allow your children to disparage ideas that we regard as holy. It would cast a gloomy shadow over their entire lives.

My devout listeners: Judaism is a religion of freedom. Among us, nobody has the right to say to another, "You no longer belong to us," as long as his views are based on the knowledge and recognition of the one God. The heavenly ladder that Jacob saw in his dream, extending from the earth to the heavens, was, according to the pronouncement of our sages, sixty thousand miles wide, to indicate that God is readily accessible to all who aspire to recognize Him and draw close to Him. This will lead, by itself, to the recognition of זה א-לי ואנוהו א-להי אבי וארממנהו, "This is my God and I will glorify Him, the God of my father and I will exalt Him." It should be our most sacred aspiration to see our children deeply immersed in the knowledge of our forefathers' religion and to recognize its sublime worth. Their love and interest for what is holy should make them feel intimately at one with the belief of their forefathers.

My devout listeners: We are about to begin a solemn and mournful part of our service. We see the images of our dearly departed appearing before us, as heartfelt prayers for the welfare of their souls spring forth from our lips. Sleeping gently in the great beyond, they have the unshakable confidence that we, their survivors, are thinking of them in our houses of worship at this sacred hour. Indeed, there is something joyous and uplifting in the awareness that they maintain a permanent place in the hearts of those they left behind. This tender feeling is uniquely a part of the words that Israel uttered at the Red Sea: א-להי אבי וארממנהו, "I will exalt the God of my fathers." For when the bond with the fatherly religion is severed, if the son and daughter no longer consider holy that which was holy for their parents, a breach between the hearts ensues, creating a gaping gulf. Piety is the darling daughter of religion; when one disappears, the other will not long remain. Piety shines so long as it is touched by a ray from the outer world and illuminates man's eyes.

Only one who is indifferent – and who could possibly be indifferent? – to his children remembering him, in love and sadness, when green grass covers him, would willingly sever those bonds that unite Jewish families beyond the grave. But he who wishes his children to remember him, as he remembers those who have gone to their eternal rest before him, must ensure that the belief in God finds firm roots in the hearts of his children, and that they choose as their life's motto: א-להי אבי וארממנהו – I too will exalt the God of my fathers. Amen.

The Significance of the Revelation

First Day Shavuot 5661 [1901]

My devoted listeners: The significance of today's festival, and thus the significance of the revelation at Mount Sinai that the festival of Shavuot commemorates, is beautifully mirrored in an edifying Midrashic exegesis of our sages. With judicious wording, the Midrash describes that God planned the creation of the world with the firm and lasting proviso that its permanence would depend on Israel's acceptance of the Torah and their obligation to maintain and disseminate it. If circumstance would prove otherwise, the world would revert back to the void from which the Creator's word had made it come into being (Talmud Bavli, *Avodah Zarah* 5a).

Israel did, indeed, accept the Torah. And on that day, millennia ago at the foot of Mount Sinai, they declared themselves ready to accept the mission for which they were destined by their Creator, and they thereby experienced the Revelation. Thus was the world assured that it would endure.

But it was not the physical, visible world of which the Midrash spoke, but rather the moral permanence of humanity. Without the support of God's revealed Law, mankind could not survive. Without the faith in God showing him the way to perfection and ennoblement, man would fall prey to ruin and decay. The animals, to be sure, have not changed since God's word called them into being, only because they are subject to the laws with which His wisdom imbued them. Why then could mankind not have been governed in the same way? Because that which makes human beings what they are – that which elevates them above all other creatures and affords them a special place in nature – was bestowed on them by religion, and it is religion that preserves man, as was guaranteed at Sinai.

With fanciful imagery our sages pictured this wonderful, unforgettable phenomenon, which Scripture painted with but a few broad strokes, the very brevity of its description exerting an all the more powerful effect on us. Our sages portrayed for us the giving of the Law. When God revealed His Torah, His call reverberated to the ends of the earth. Mighty nations became terrified and trembled. With great trepidation they came to Balaam, the heathen prophet, to learn from him the meaning of this singular event.

"Does God, perchance, wish to destroy the universe again? Will a great deluge inundate the earth, as in earlier times, and destroy all living things? The destruction of all life did once occur, as God, in His anger, washed away all existence. As happened then, can ruin and death set in once again?"

But Balaam calmed them: "Rest assured, God will not destroy His creation. He invests it with stability and support, lending it radiance, majesty, and beauty, because He has transmitted to His people a priceless gift, the Torah, which is called עז, 'strength,' and this will be a blessing for Israel and for all of us."

When the nations heard this, they united in a joyful cry: ה׳ עז לעמו יתן ה׳ יברך את עמו בשלום, "God gives strength unto His people, God blesses His people with peace" (Psalms 29:11). Peace shall be yours, O Israel, on your coming in, peace shall be yours on your going out, peace shall reign on all of mankind.

In this most engaging manner did our sages give expression to the significance of the Revelation for Israel and for all of humanity, that it be a blessing for all. In choosing, therefore, a theme by which to contemplate the meaning of this festival of Shavuot, none is more worthy than that which will bring to us a clear awareness of the significance of the Revelation at Mount Sinai.

My devout listeners: When we hear today loud voices speaking in derogatory fashion concerning the merits and meaning of our faith, we might readily come to believe that the beneficent influence on the development and progress of humanity that we ascribe to our Torah is but a figment of our imagination. Not the slightest credit is given to us. Instead, concepts that had, until now, been the undisputed products of Jewish spiritual life are contested by means of distortion and misrepresentation, and the beneficial effects to mankind attributed to Judaism's daughter religion.

We would certainly be the last to deny the beneficial effect that the daughter religion has exerted on the development of human culture, or to seek to belittle its splendid successes. We would not be so shortsighted as to see only good on one side and nothing of significance on the other side. When, however, we hear today that the Christian way of life is the only one that is valid – when Christianity is represented as the only religion bringing salvation to mankind while Judaism's teachings, though they may have had some value in their time, are now totally antiquated – then we vigorously raise our voices at this misreading of historical facts and this distortion of our holy literature. Well we know that our voices do not reach into the outer world, especially not in those circles where any credit we deserve for building human civilization is being denied to us. And yet we must not remain silent in the face of such calumny, which even appears in the newspapers. Most importantly, we Jews must remain fully aware of the purity and majesty of our faith, and to survey our blessed life, which the warm rays of our religion's sun have brought to such splendid growth.

What was the state of humanity before Abraham unfurled the banner of one single God and placed his descendents at His service, long before the everlasting foundations of morality and justice were given at Sinai? How was our world before the voices of our prophets resonated in advocating the recognition of our holy God on high, and the acceptance of His code of morality here on earth? There are, to be sure, civilizations older than the Jews. Already when Abraham left Mesopotamia, there were nations with well-advanced civilizations. And when he arrived in Egypt he found there a people quite distinguished in wisdom and art. But all these ancient peoples who had achieved so much – be it in the field of art and science, in establishing nations, or in the politics of worldly affairs – had no understanding for that most sublime question of life, namely, what really moves the human heart. Their concept of God and of the value and purpose of human existence was thoroughly distorted.

It was not till Israel appeared in the annals of history that mankind received a new message. Israel established a permanent place on earth for morality and the worship of God. Its teachings turned people into human beings by elevating them above the profane, tearing them away from the abyss of transience, and uniting them with eternity. ברא הקב"ה את העליונים לעליונים ואת התחתונים לתחתונים, ובא משה ועשה את העליונים לתחתונים ואת התחתונים לעליונים – "Heaven and earth had always been separated. The Eternal formed a kingdom for Himself, while the earthly creatures lived their earthly lives. Then came Moses and reversed the former order: he brought the heavens down to earth and led man upward to the heavens" (*Yalkut Shimoni Yehoshua* 20).

Indeed, mankind owes its heavenly blessings and bond with God and eternity to the transmission of Israel's heritage. From the summit of Sinai rose the sun that, today, lends spiritual comfort and nourishment to all of mankind. To Israel came the call: "I am the Eternal, your God, most holy, loving, and everlasting," which Israel, by means of its Bible, made known to all of the nations. Israel, despite the hostility of opposing nations, raised the banner of law for mankind, thereby laying the foundation for the promotion of love of fellow man. Israel established the principle that men are created in the image of God, and that oppression and enslavement of one's fellow man is therefore forbidden.

To be sure, were we to believe the unkind utterances of our adversaries, we might conclude that our religion has achieved nothing, that it was the daughter religion, or perhaps the old Teutons, who first bestowed their blessings on mankind. The masses might be led astray, but we Jews are not confused about our faith. We know that thousands of years before a son of our people emphasized the principle of "Love thy neighbor as thyself" as man's primary duty, Moses had already demanded this of his people, and Hillel, that wise teacher of the Law, had established it as the foundation of our faith. No one can dispute that the sublime doctrines of human freedom and nobility are the spiritual products of our people. We testify, by simply referring to God's Book, that care for the poor, the weak, and the needy bears the stamp of Judaism. So listen, you nations: the torch of human kindness, which has extended to the farthest corner of the earth, was lit by the spiritual rays of the Sinaic Law. The concept of everlasting peace on earth is derived from the prophets of Israel, and the message of the brotherhood of man has its source in Jewish writings.

We have emphasized this not at all with the idea of boasting, but rather so that we should be thoroughly imbued with the grandeur and superiority of our faith, which others seek to disparage. No, we do not take pride in the great contribution Israel has made in lending mankind nobility and morality; rather, we consider it as the fulfillment of our duty, the carrying out of the historic mission that God assigned to us. Although we do consider it a historic fact that God chose Israel, and assigned to us a mission higher and nobler than was given to any other nation, yet we do not claim to stand at a higher level or be more worthy in the eyes of God than others. It is rather that we have taken upon ourselves far-reaching duties and more lofty goals.

With their ingenious portrayal, our sages tell us that God offered the Torah to different nations (*Rashi*, Deuteronomy 33:2), who, on hearing that the Torah demands restraint and self-control and that evil lust and wanton impulses must be subdued, refused to accept it. Only Israel submitted to its demands, with soulful fervor and enthusiasm. The invocation of the name of the Almighty with veneration and devout prayer to Him, as well as rendering love to our fellow man – all this emanated directly or indirectly from Israel and from the revelation at Sinai.

My devout listeners: When our forefathers of yore dwelled in the land of Palestine, our festival of Shavuot was also a festival of harvest – the festival of the first fruit. A grateful multitude brought the first fruit up to the Temple in pious homage to God. In our country and our climate, this festival always occurs at springtime, with its splendor and its fragrant blossoms. My devout listeners: the time is yet remote when we will be able to celebrate Shavuot also as a harvest festival in its spiritual sense, when Israel will reap what it has sown over the millennia, when the belief in one God and His moral code instilled into mankind will bring magnificent fruits that will be a source of spiritual sustenance, when the nations will readily acknowledge the debt they owe to Israel, and give us our full due of justice.

May this festival ever be for us a time of blossoming, that it will flourish because of our fear of the Lord and loyalty to our faith. May we be blessed with the thought expressed in the book of Psalms (19:8): תורת ה׳ תמימה משיבת נפש, "The Law of the Lord is perfect, restoring the soul." Amen.

Honor Your Father and Mother

Second Day Shavuot 5660 [1900]

Whereas we spoke yesterday, the first day of Shavuot, concerning the significance of the revelation on Mount Sinai and the demands that this enormous event has placed upon the Jewish people, let us focus today upon one of the Ten Commandments. Once again I choose the Fifth Commandment, even though it was the topic of my sermon only a year ago, because this commandment speaks to the innermost part of our hearts:

כבד את אביך ואת אמך למען יארכון ימיך
על האדמה אשר ה' א-להיך נתן לך.

Honor your father and your mother so that your days may be lengthened upon the land which the Lord your God gives you."
(Exodus 20:12)

Can we ever talk to children too much about their parents? In this hour, when many of you remember your departed parents, while others gaze heavenward in gratitude that they still enjoy the support of their parents, can we hear enough about what fills our hearts? Today, however, I would like to consider the Fifth Commandment from a new perspective, especially its position vis-à-vis the other commandments on the stone tablets. The reality of the Revelation makes it clear that the order of the commandments provides us with a special lesson that we should take to heart.

My devout listeners: It is the commandment of אנכי ה' א-להיך, "I am the Lord your God" (Exodus 20:2), that introduces the Divine proclamation. The Midrash relates that these words had the effect of a mighty thunderclap convulsing the earth. All lands shuddered before it, the nations trembled, and the pagan gods were toppled from their thrones into the dust. And when the kings of the world heard this call and the subsequent commandments, all of which expressed reverence for God, they thought maliciously: The God of Israel is only concerned that people worship Him, watching jealously that no one worship other gods besides Him. When, however, they heard an equally mighty voice resounding from Mount Sinai saying, "Honor your father and your mother," their slanderous tongue was silenced, and they, too, bowed humbly before the majesty of the first declaration of אנכי (Talmud Bavli, *Kiddushin* 31a).

Indeed, my devout listeners, it is not without significance that the commandment of loving one's parents has its place on the first of the two tablets. It follows immediately those commandments concerned with the worship of the one God, because reverence for the Heavenly Father above is intimately related to the respect we give to our parents. This juxtaposition of the commandments provides a profound lesson for parents, as well as a wake-up call for their children! The parental home is the most certain path toward religious development. By teaching as well as by example, the child receives the strongest motivation for his religious thinking and feeling. Therefore, parents, if you wish to discharge your obligations toward your Creator, be not satisfied merely to serve God faithfully, to carry a pious heart in your breast, and cherish sacred love for your belief and religion. That Divine light that illuminates your life must also be kindled in your children, steering their hearts to sanctity, bolstering their belief in God and their attachment to His teachings. Only then will you have demonstrated the true sincerity of your belief in God.

Our sages tell us that when God wanted to reveal Himself, He asked Israel for assurance that they would eagerly follow His precepts. It was only after Israel offered their children as guarantors for the upholding of God's commandments that the Almighty gave them His Torah (*Song of Songs Rabbah* 1:4). We too must offer assurance that the keeping of God's commandments will ever be the highest priority for us. It is only our children, however, who can be our true guarantors. For that reason we must educate them in the knowledge and practice of our religion, and train them to become potent advocates of our belief. Only then can they ensure Israel's future and the perpetuation of our Law.

And yet, this Fifth Commandment, both in its wording as well as in its relationship to the other commandments, is primarily directed to the children. Significantly, the commandment is "honor" – not "love" – your father and mother, since respect for father and mother is more than affection and love. It must be intimately connected to the preceding commandments. The worship of God should be the stimulus leading to the veneration of parents. On the other hand, the instinctive feelings toward parents should be the fertile ground for the tree of life of our faith. השוה הכתוב מוראת אב ואם למוראת המקום, "Scripture has equated reverence for God with reverence for one's parents" (Talmud Bavli, *Kiddushin* 30b). The two are intimately connected and they have a reciprocal relationship. We learn in the Talmud: "Three have a share in every human being: his father, his mother, and the Holy One up above. God opens His abode to him who honors his parents and regards him as honoring God Himself" (Talmud Bavli, *Niddah* 31a). Thus Israel's reverence toward parents has always been intimately tied to the reverence for God. Reverence for one's parents should include not only honoring their personage but also respect for those things that they hold sacred. Jewish survival, in spite of centuries of hatred by the nations of the world, rests, in no small measure, on this principle.

One might well ask whether reverence for one's parents precludes entertaining thoughts and sensibilities that run counter to those the parents espouse, dismissing any and every independent religious thought. Such objections are not infrequently put forth, and they may indeed become the motivation to embark on a lifestyle that is not at all in keeping with their parents' wishes. But softly! You sons and daughters, do not be too clever! Try to appreciate your parents' religious feelings, whose strength lies in their connection to the earlier generations. Consider carefully whether those things that were dear to our parents would not also be worthy of our esteem.

Allow me to tell you: he who has truly immersed himself in the knowledge of our belief and familiarized himself with the essence of our religion – he might perhaps come to regard the religious truths from a point of view that differs from that of his parents. While he might see his relationship with his parents in a different way, he will nevertheless declare, as Moses and the

Children of Israel did at the Red Sea: א-להי אבי וארממנהו, "The God of my fathers, I will exalt Him" (Exodus 15:2). The religious treasures transmitted to him by his ancestors will remain for him sublime and holy, because they contain unalloyed truths and are permeated with light and clarity. Only in rare instances will mature thinking and clear insight cause discord between the religious feelings of parents and those of their children. More often it is only cheap catch words and circumlocution that are used to pass judgment on the most venerable matters.

Granted that respect for one's parents can be demonstrated during their lifetime without the help of religion, and such respect should certainly not cease with their passing away. However, a close relationship between the living and their departed parents can only be maintained via the medium of religion. Neither flowers nor wreaths nor showy funeral processions with external expressions of grief constitute true piety. A more exalted and noble form of piety manifests itself when religion seeks to form a bond between the yearning of the living and the departed souls of their dear ones – when faith soars into the pure spheres of eternity, and we can yet feel, beyond all the pain and suffering, united with those whose image fills our souls. Is it not most touching when the religious Jew, long after his year of mourning and even into his very old age, is beckoned to the house of God on the *yahrzeit* day, once again to pray that his dearly departed be remembered? Even with the passage of decades, the love for the departed is not extinguished, but is rather strengthened from year to year.

My devout listeners: The Midrash relates that following the building of the Tabernacle in the desert, as Moses was about to announce the order in which the tribes were to be positioned around the Tabernacle, the great leader became very despondent and with great trepidation spoke to the Eternal: "O, Master, will there not arise discord and strife among the tribes with the announcement of how they will be positioned, each desiring the other's location?"

But God reassured his troubled servant, saying, "You will not be required to arrange the order of the tribes. The people of Israel possess the testament of their patriarch Jacob, ordaining that when, in the future, the position and order of the tribes around the Tabernacle be delineated, it will be in the same order as when the sons of Jacob accompanied his body from Egypt back to the Holy Land" (*Yalkut Shimoni Bamidbar* 685). Indeed, this marvelous image that the Midrash portrays for us retains its full validity today. As children stand before the bier of their parents and render them honor, so do they stand before God.

O, my devout listeners: You feel in this sad hour, more than my feeble words can express, what it means to extend honor to those who are departed. You now appreciate that religion and prayer have the capacity to form an invisible bond between you, living here on earth, and those up above, to whom your thoughts now turn. Their spirit seems to have descended down to you, and you have been lifted up to them. Now you will recognize the intimate connection between the commandments bidding us to honor God and the commandment to honor our parents – that is, the relationship between religion and piety.

May your experiences in this hour exert their effect on how you conduct your lives, and may you take to heart, in thought and in deed, these instructions to honor God and to honor your parents. Amen.

I, THE LORD, AM YOUR GOD

First Day Shavuot and Confirmation, 5663 [1903]

תקרב רנתי לפניך ה׳.
May our prayers be pleasing unto You, O Lord. (Psalms 119:169)

As we recall that exalted event at Mount Sinai, where Israel heard the proclamation of Your Law, we approach You today to dedicate ourselves to Your lofty service. May the spirit of our ancestors also descend upon us, and may You look with favor at our deeds.

Therefore have these youngsters come here today to declare, in this sacred abode and in the presence of this holy congregation, what bestirs their hearts, that they will be faithful unto You and ever be dedicated to You.

Look down on all of us with favor, strengthen our resolve, and consecrate our deeds, so that we may dedicate our lives to Your Honor and find happiness therein. Amen.

My devoted festive assembly: The event that we are celebrating today – can any tongue describe it fully, or any mouth express its true significance? It has been celebrated in song throughout the millennia, recorded with rapture-evoking imagination. The harp tones of the psalmist declared the praise of Him Who revealed Himself on this day. The powerful orations of the prophets were but an echo of the message given to Israel at Mount Sinai. The poetic wisdom of word and image that emanated from the Revelation was the truth that was transmitted in plain and simple language to the great masses. And all the wise and learned men, who toiled in the building of our literature, merely explained and expanded on what had been transmitted to them by Moses.

And yet, the message from Sinai continues to sprout forth new buds and blossoms. The fountainhead that originated at Horeb continues to widen more and more, irrigating distant lands in the course of time and flooding the channels of culture and history. This might also explain the lively discussion recently engendered in the cultural world, which centered on how the message of the Revelation was disseminated, via the Jewish people, to all of mankind. The mystical aura attributed to the Jews by the nations, and their prominent place in history, was seen as having developed not as a Divine gift but along natural lines. The blossoming of human spiritual life was felt to have emanated from Babylon. That everlasting blessing that Israel has, to this day, defiantly defended, was believed to have evolved out of the chaos of crude heathen concepts of belief.

And yet, we do not regret this discussion. We are confident that it will only contribute to the enhancement of the truth of our Torah. Such discussion makes us appreciate the significance that resides in our holy literature and the beneficial effect it has on all of humanity. We will come to the realization that today's cultural life is founded on the bedrock of our Torah. And should one presume that the tablets of Sinai can be replaced by a few clay slabs recovered from centuries-old ruins – we know the truth with absolute certainty: the dusty clouds of Babylonian excavations will never darken the sun of Sinai. We rejoice in the precious words inscribed on the two tablets of the covenant, words that illuminate our hearts, words whose validity remains eternal. We know that it was the proclamation at Mount Sinai that liberated Israel from the delusions of the idol worship, which was so popular in ancient times. It was the Revelation that separated us from the other nations and directed our path heavenward.

The very first word of God's covenant conveys to us this triumphant certainty, breaching for all time the religious beliefs of the heathen world, and guaranteeing that God's message will remain eternal. Let us, today, examine more carefully the meaning of these words.

אנכי ה׳ א-להיך אשר הוצאתיך מארץ מצרים מבית עבדים, "I am the Lord your God, Who has taken you out of the land of Egypt from the house of bondage" (Exodus 20:2). Thus sounded the first Divine call to Israel. Thereby God revealed Himself not just to Moses and Aaron, or to a few chosen people in high places. Divine revelation extended to the entire people, old and young, the powerful and the lowly, and this is what lends this phenomenon its significance. Our religious teachings did not become the domain of an all-powerful, secret priestly sect, but rather, the property of the entire people.

It was a double message that Israel received on Mount Sinai: "I am the Lord" and "I am the Lord your God." I am the Lord, the eternal Ruler, the eternal Being. I am He Who is eternal and remains eternal, I alone – none else. This call is also directed to those who presume that God shares His kingdom with other beings, that there are other supernatural powers besides Him. This message, as the Midrash relates, reached out to the four corners of the earth, its ring causing all idols to crash into the dust.

If it were true indeed that the holy name of the God of Israel had been known in Babylon, it would hardly have mattered, since He would have been represented only as a god among many others, with many of the heathen characteristics attributed to Him. The Lord, the one and only, the pure spiritual God of heaven and earth, Who guides the fate of man according to His wise and benevolent plans – it was this God whom Israel first came to know at Mount Sinai.

Abraham had already recognized the true God, Whom he trusted and to Whom he was drawn in confidence. Before Abraham, Noah's flawless way of life found favor in God's eyes, and Enoch was transformed by Him. But in no way does this diminish the significance of the message of Sinai. We read in the second book of Moses: "I appeared to Abraham, Isaac, and Jacob as the Almighty God, but by the name Adonai I was not known by them" (Exodus 6:3). God was known in former days as the almighty and omnipotent Creator of the world, whose sublime throne was in the upper heights. Now, Israel came to know Him as Adonai, infinitely good, infinitely loving, who descends down to those in need, and who draws man toward Him through mercy and love. It was at Mount Sinai that Israel came to recognize God in His holy perfection.

Our sages, with characteristic symbolic language, say that the mountains of Tabor and Carmel rushed over upon hearing the words אנכי ה' א-להיך, "I am the Lord your God," in order to listen to the proclamation (see also Targum, Psalms 68). But when they heard the words: אשר הוצאתיך מארץ מצרים מבית עבדים, "Who has taken you out of the land of Egypt, from the house of bondage," they turned around and went back. This indicates that Israel should not conclude from this Sinaitic proclamation that God holds sway over nature and rules over the entire world. That had already been recognized by Abraham and other enlightened men, perhaps even in Babylon. Here God established with Israel an intimate relationship, and via Israel with all of mankind. The message to humanity was that man is not a lost, neglected limb within the bustle of this world. Divine rays crown his forehead, lifting him beyond this earthly life and binding him to eternity.

God's message, as our sages relate, reached every individual, each according to his status and his level of comprehension. To the aged, it appeared as the fruit of mature life experience; to the mature, strong words of encouragement; and for the youngster, glowing enthusiasm and lofty flights of thought. For children it was stimulating and encouraging. Yes, the call reached each and every member of the people of Israel: I, Adonai, sublime and all-embracing, am your God. I know what animates you, understand all your feelings and sentiments, and anticipate, with this My message, your heart's most urgent needs and prayers.

Indeed, it is the everlasting blessing of the Revelation that brought Israel to the realization that God's rule is not limited to the realm of the stars, but that He is the benevolent Father of each and every one of us; in Him we find refuge from all of life's tribulations, and safety in His protection. This gives God's word at Sinai its incomparable eminence and assures its everlasting existence. And even if, after the passage of millennia, the world will once again be dug out from under its rubble and confront Israel's Revelation – never will the message from Sinai be eclipsed. Even in the distant future, God's word will illuminate man's path and lead him from the darkness to spiritual heights.

I therefore wish to lead you too, my dear students, in your mind's imagination, to Mount Sinai, so that God's message may reverberate to you in all its significance. Just as Moses exhorted Israel to remain loyal to God's commandments with the words כי הוא חייך וארך ימיך, "For it is your life and the length of your days" (Deuteronomy 30:20), so do I wish to show you today that your faithfulness to God and His commandments will lead you to greater happiness and a more exalted view of life.

Our sages tell us that God created two angels to accompany each and every member of the people of Israel when He made His Torah known to them (Talmud Bavli, *Shabbat* 88a). For you also did God create these two angels: one angel to watch over you, the other to guide you. Because he who has heard the message from Sinai and directs his heart toward God, he walks on sacred ground, and is protected from outside as well as from within, from envy, temptation, and slander.

You have thus far led tranquil lives, watched over by the caring eyes of your dear parents who have kept you away from all unhappy experiences. Your parents will continue lovingly to guard your footsteps and direct your future along the right path. But life can be sober, especially in our time, and doubly so for us who acknowledge the one and only God. You will therefore need firm conviction, faith, and enthusiasm in your belief, which you can achieve only through an intimate bond with the faith of our forefathers.

"I am the Lord your God." Thus did God speak to our ancestors, and thus He speaks to each of you today. God is ever at your side, and you can look, with confidence, for His help. Your awareness of God's presence will fortify you with steadfastness and courage. No one can deprive you of God's help, and the delight you will gain at worshiping Him is never threatened.

You must now continue to build on the foundation of the religious teachings that you gained in school, and to arrange your lives in accordance with the Divine will. Create within your hearts a sanctuary for God, and keep your souls pure and immaculate. Keep your unshakeable faith in God, even where personal sacrifice and self-denial is demanded of you.

"Serve the Lord with gladness, and come before Him with joyous song" (Psalms 100:1) sings the Psalter. Come here to this holy place, be it in times of sadness or in happiness. Come here on Sabbaths and on festivals, to give honor to the one and only and to direct your hearts toward Him in all of your endeavors. May today's celebration, as well the future remembrance of it, sustain you every day anew, so that this hour remain a blessing for you all the days of your lives. So may God, in His mercy, grant. Amen.

Prayer of a Student

We too implore You, benevolent God. You have been our help and support from the earliest days of our childhood, and You will never forsake us. We have learned from our religious instruction how, with unending love, You encompass all of humanity. We understand that You called upon our ancestors to be a nation of priests in order to serve Your Holy Name, with the mandate to disseminate on this earth the teachings of the one and only eternal God. We wish to demonstrate that we will always be members of that covenant which You concluded with our forefathers, to be true to You and Your holy teachings, even when temptation threatens to alienate us from You. Gladly do we proclaim in this holy place those maxims which will be our guides for the lives we have chosen. As our ancestors did at Mount Sinai, so do we now declare: כל אשר דבר ה׳ נעשה ונשמע, "All the words that the Lord has spoken, we will do and heed" (Exodus 24:7).

The students each declare their own maxims, adding an appropriate solemn vow. The rabbi directs to each individual a word of exhortation corresponding to her maxim, after which one of the students offers the following prayer:

Benevolent Father in Heaven. Accept our sincere thanks for Your kindness and love in giving us precious and loving parents who stand at our side. Their hopes for life and prosperity correspond to ours. Our hearts swell with joyful thanks to those who have to this day led us and have surrounded us with a protective wall of love. There is no better way to express our love than in this our prayer to You for their welfare: Preserve our dear benefactors for many, many years into ripe old age, protect them through Your grace, and may our fortune be theirs. Amen.

Prayer of the Rabbi

All-benevolent God, may Your countenance shine on these young ladies, that they remain true to their maxims. Imbue them with Your spirit to carry out Your word, Your word that is eternal, as You are eternal. Spread Your canopy of peace over their heads, to shield them from all harm, and bid Your angel to guard them in all their life's pathways. Implant into the hearts of their parents the firm resolve to continue building on the foundation which Your teachings have established in their children's hearts. Grant these children constant reverence for their dear parents, so that they will always feel indebted to them for their happiness and welfare.

Prayer of a Student

We also implore You, benevolent God, that you lend us strength in our resolve to carry out Your will. We seek Your guidance as we walk through life, so that Your word shall be a lamp unto our feet, a light unto our path (Psalms 119:105). Grant that we keep this promise always, never to deviate from Your ways, or lose ourselves in life's maze. We thus implore You, Almighty, from the depth of our hearts: (*all together*) יהיו לרצון אמרי פי והגיון לבי לפניך ה׳ צורי וגאלי, "May the words of my mouth and the meditation of my heart be acceptable before You, my Rock and my Redeemer" (Psalms 19:15). Amen.

Closing Words of the Rabbi

קרוב ה׳ לכל קראיו לכל אשר יקראהו באמת – "The Lord is close to all that call upon Him, to all that call upon Him in truth" (Psalms 145:18). So will God always be close to you, when you call Him in truth. And now לכו לשלום, go in peace and preserve the memory of this celebration in order to maintain faithfully your sacred pledge. May the eternal God grant you strength in this undertaking, and bestow upon you His blessing:

יברכך ה׳ וישמרך, יאר ה׳ פניו אליך ויחנך, ישא ה׳ פניו אליך וישם לך שלום – "The Lord bless you and keep you. The Lord cause His countenance to shine upon You and be gracious unto you. The Lord lift up His countenance unto you and grant you peace." (Numbers 6:24–26). Amen.